Y0-DFH-667

Flexography Primer

by
Donna C. Mulvihill

Graphic Arts Technical Foundation
4615 Forbes Avenue
Pittsburgh, Pennsylvania 15213
United States of America
Telephone: 412/621-6941
Telex: 866412   Cable: GATFWORLD

Foundation of Flexographic
Technical Association
95 West Nineteenth Street
Huntington Station, New York 11746
United States of America
Telephone: 516/271-4538
Telex: 971328

Copyright © 1985
Graphic Arts Technical Foundation

Library of Congress Catalog Card Number: 85-70601
International Standard Book Number: 0-88362-076-6

Printed in the United States of America

Contents

Chapter	Title	Page
1	Development of Flexography	1
2	Image Preparation	17
3	Flexographic Plates	29
4	Flexographic Presses	41
5	Flexographic Substrates	55
6	Flexographic Inks	65
7	Converting/Finishing	75
8	Flexography's Future	85
	Glossary	91
	Index	103

Foreword

This book is one of a series being developed to introduce the basics of the five major printing processes—flexography, gravure, letterpress, lithography, and screen printing. The relative importance of each of these printing processes has varied with the passing years, but today all five distinctively different processes flourish and compete. Yet each has its own advantages for particular uses.

The five primers of this GATF series on printing processes are designed for a variety of audiences:
• Students who want or require an introduction to one or more of the printing processes. For students not primarily concerned with graphic arts, or with the specific process, this may constitute the entire study of the particular area covered by the book. For others, it may be an introduction to more advanced study of the area.
• Industrial persons not in the graphic arts but who deal with the printing industry: artists who do work for other areas as well as for graphic arts reproduction purposes; print buyers; printing equipment and supplies manufacturers and salespeople; publishers; and researchers who touch on printing.
• Industrial persons in graphic arts organizations, but not in areas directly related to production: salespeople, accountants, secretaries; and even people related to production who are in specialties—particularly those newly practicing these specialties in graphic arts situations—such as those in materials handling, quality control, engineering, maintenance, and estimating.
• Persons in a very narrow niche within a graphic arts production process—say folder operating—who are ambitious to have a broader understanding of the other areas of the process beyond their own work.
• Persons working in one process of printing—even those with broad understanding of the whole process—who want to learn something about one or more other processes. This includes managers and workers who are beginning to think about installing another process from the one or ones they are familiar with.
• Anybody who would simply like to know something about one or more printing processes, quite apart from any present or future work in or related to it.

Raymond N. Blair
Editor-in-Chief

1 Development of Flexography

Flexography is a graphic arts reproduction process that derives its name from the flexible printing plates it employs. The term "graphic" refers to pictures and writing.

THE BEGINNING OF GRAPHIC COMMUNICATIONS

Development of Graphics

The earliest known pictures were drawings found on cave walls. The characters for writing were developed from simplified pictures or symbols called **pictographs.** Particular pictographs and their combinations called **ideograms** were used to express ideas as well as objects. Early civilizations developed elaborate systems of ideographic writing. The Chinese system, for example, with its thousands of ideograms, has persisted into modern times.

Among other peoples the evolution continued from ideographic writing to **phonetic writing,** where the symbols came to represent sounds. In some languages, like the Egyptian, each symbol represented the sound of a whole syllable. In others, like the European, each symbol came to represent a basic element of sound. This **alphabetic system** required the fewest different symbols, or characters.

EARLY WRITING SURFACES AND MATERIALS

From the first-used natural surfaces of cave walls, cliffs, boulders, stones, and bones, mankind progressed by shaping and smoothing these natural materials and developing new ones on which to record their histories, laws, literature, business records, teachings, and other communications.

The Babylonians and Assyrians used clay tablets for their permanent records. They punched wedge-shaped marks with a stylus into soft clay, which was then baked so hard that some of the tablets still exist. The ancient Egyptian scribes wrote with red and black inks and tufted reed pens on sheets of **papyrus,** the forerunner of paper, made from the papyrus plant.

The Egyptians were using tanned animal hide as a writing material by 2000 B.C., but this didn't become a serious contender until it had been developed into a very fine material called **parchment.** Gradually, over many centuries, papyrus was completely superseded by parchment, which in turn was replaced by paper.

Paper, made of water-suspended cellulose fibers from various sources (originally old fabrics and sometimes fish nets, tree bark, etc.) had been invented by the Chinese about the end of the first century A.D. During the next 400 years its use spread throughout China. Its

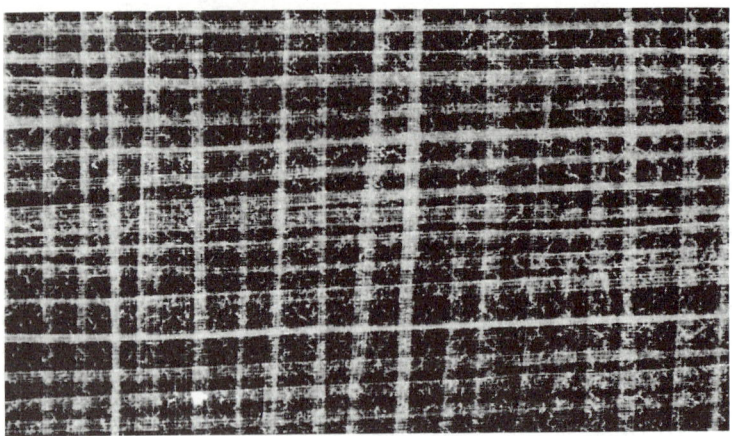

Papyrus stalks were cut into long, tissue-thin sections to fabricate the lattice-like structure of paper.

use in Europe grew very slowly because of the great superiority of parchment quality to that of the early European paper. The scribes of Europe were busy copying and recopying book manuscripts on **vellum,** a fine type of parchment made from calfskin.

THE INVENTION OF PRINTING

The endless recopying of books by scribes was rendered unnecessary by the invention of **typographic printing** (printing from individual,

Before Johann Gutenberg popularized the use of cast-metal types, they were hand-carved from wood.

Development of Flexography 5

movable types, using a press) in Germany in the mid-fifteenth century. The idea of somehow mechanically reproducing writing instead of manually copying it had been experimented with in earlier centuries. The Chinese in the ninth century, and probably much earlier, were printing from full-page wooden blocks. But apparently none of the Oriental experimenters considered the use of a press.

Johann Gutenberg and his contemporaries in Germany employed individual cast-metal types and a press to begin a printing industry that spread into all parts of the world, and has continued to the present.

Printing at the end of the fifteenth century consisted of:
- a set of steel dies (**patrices**) with characters cut out in relief,
- character molds (**matrices**) punched into copper with the steel dies,
- many identical characters formed by repeatedly pouring a molten

A typecase *(top)*, or California Job Case, as it is called, stores individual types. Hand-held composing sticks *(right)* were used when assembling type into words and lines. Then the lines were transferred to a tray called a galley *(left)*. Also pictured are Linotype matrices *(bottom center)* and single lines of type cast in hot metal.

lead alloy into the character mold,
- a typecase for storing the individual types in specific compartments,
- a composing stick for holding the types as they were placed manually one after another in lines spaced out (by adjusting spaces between words) to even lengths and sometimes separated by thin lead strips,

6   Flexography Primer

ffi	fl	5 EM	4 EM	,	k		1	2	3	4	5	6	7	8		$	£		Æ	Œ	æ	œ
j ?	b	c	d		e				i		s		f	g	ff fi	9 0	A	B	C	D	E	F	G
! l z	l	m	n		h		o		y	p	w	^ ,	EN QUAD	EM QUAD		H	I	K	L	M	N	O
x q	v	u	t	3 EM SPACES			a		r		; .	: -	QUAD			P X	Q Y	R Z	S J	T U	V &	W ffl

Type arrangement in the California Job Case.

· metal frames in which pages of type were fixed into place, creating a **typeform,**
· a press with a flat surface **(bed)** on which the typeform was placed,

*Courtesy Cover & Text Paper Manufacturers,
American Paper Institute, Inc.*

Gutenberg examining a page of his fifteenth-century Bible masterpiece.

inked, and covered with a sheet of paper, and a movable upper flat surface **(platen)** that was pressed down firmly upon the paper. Printing continued in this form for 400 years after Gutenberg.

Because this system transferred ink from raised letters to paper on a press, it came to be known as **letterpress.**

DEVELOPMENT OF THE PRESS

The press was the part of the printing process that evolved fastest. The invention of printing stabilized the basic forms of letters (which had varied erratically during the times of the scribes), so that some

Development of Flexography 7

Keyboard-operated Linotype casts one-piece lines of type in hot metal.

typefaces designed centuries ago are much like those commonly used today. The nature of type and the typesetting process didn't change drastically until the invention of the **Linotype** and **Monotype,** mechanical typecasting machines, in the late nineteenth century, and the

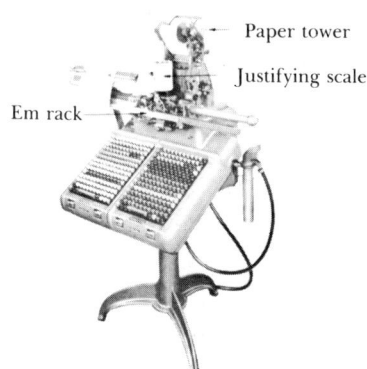

Monotype keyboard. This tape-driven typesetting machine is used in conjunction with the Monotype caster.

Monotype caster.

twentieth-century development of **phototypesetting,** which completely abandoned movable three-dimensional types on which letterpress originally had been based.

But the press, made of wood and apparently first adapted in design from preexisting wine or manuscript bookbinding presses, underwent steady improvement. The rapid increase in the use of books, pamphlets, magazines, and newspapers made possible by letterpress printing stimulated the development of faster, more efficient equipment.

Since raising the platen with the original wooden worm screw high enough to insert the leather inking pad and then lowering it with pressure on the next sheet was time-consuming, a movable bed that could be drawn out for inking and slid back into place for the next impression was invented. The wooden worm screw was redesigned and later replaced with an iron mechanism during the mid-sixteenth century. A counterweight was installed to lift the platen automatically early in the seventeenth century. And by the end of the eighteenth century, the whole press body was built of metal.

Over time, many productivity improvements were made that gradually replaced up-and-down, back-and-forth movements of press components with continuous, rotational movements. First came the **inking roller,** a leather-covered cylinder (end of eighteenth century). Near the beginning of the nineteenth century, a press was devised with an impression cylinder that replaced the platen. As it rotated, it carried a sheet of paper into contact with the inked typeform affixed to a flatbed moving back and forth. The cylinder and the flatbed were synchronized during the impression cycle but the cylinder was lifted from the flatbed as the type was carried back under the inking rollers. Soon, steam power began to be applied to these flatbed-cylinder presses.

Eliminating the back-and-forth motion of the flatbed in order to have a fully rotary press required the replacement of the flat typeform with a cylinder also. A system was tried briefly that held the type on the surface of a cylinder—which (along with paper fed from rolls instead of a stack of sheets) made the rotary system complete. But the type sometimes fell off the cylinder, and better printing cylinder techniques evolved for rotary letterpress. Meanwhile, completely different printing processes had been developed for which the cylindrical printing surface was exceptionally well suited.

NONLETTERPRESS PRINTING PROCESSES

Printing processes are classified by the way their printing surfaces accept ink on areas that are to print **(image areas)** and reject it on the other areas **(nonimage areas).** The image area surfaces in letterpress are raised above the nonimage areas and thus are the only ones touched by the inking apparatus.

In another process, **lithography,** a level surface is processed photochemically to make the image areas attractive to a greasy ink and the nonimage areas, when dampened, repellent to greasy ink. The printing surface material now commonly used is a coated flexible aluminum, easily curved around the printing cylinder. Modern

Development of Flexography

Courtesy Latmer & Mayer Printers & Lithographers

In letterpress, the image-area surfaces are raised above the nonimage-areas.

In offset lithography, the plate cylinder *(top)* transfers the ink to a rubber-covered cylinder called a blanket cylinder *(bottom)*, and then to the paper.

lithography, called **offset lithography,** prints first on a rubber blanket, a rubber-covered cylinder, and then transfers the image to the paper.

In a third process, **gravure,** the images are etched below the nonimage surface in the form of tiny sunken cells. The surface is bathed in ink, which enters the cells, and the surface ink is scraped off by a blade. The cylindrical form is so well suited to gravure—for etching and for rotating in a fountain of ink and against the ink-scraping blade—that practically all gravure is rotary gravure, and is called **rotogravure.**

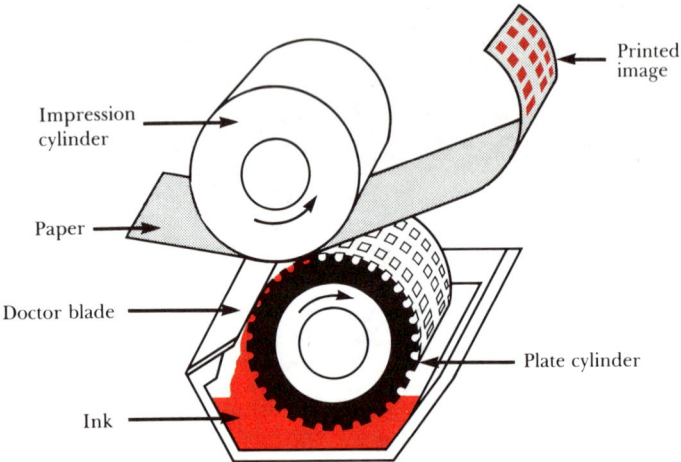

In gravure, the ink is carried in miniature recessed cells on the cylinder. Excess ink is scraped off with a blade. Ink is transferred when the cylinder contacts the surface to be printed.

ROTARY LETTERPRESS PLATES

Rotary letterpress also developed practicable printing cylinders by making solid, curved plates from the flat typeform. One such plate was the **stereotype,** which came to be widely used in newspaper printing. A pasteboard impression was made of the typeform. This, fixed inside a cylindrical form, became the mold for a lead alloy plate. A similar, higher-quality cylindrical plate was the **electrotype.** The electrotype relief plate is made by making a hot plastic or wax mold of the typeform, electroplating the mold with a coating of copper or nickel, curving the plate into a cylinder, and making it strong and rigid with a cast backing material. Thus, cylindrical plates molded from the flat typeform developed, in one direction, into higher-quality, more expensive kinds. In another direction, an inexpensive alternative became possible: the molded rubber plate.

ANILINE PRINTING

Introduced into the U.S. from Europe in the early 1900s, rotary letterpress printing that used rubber or other flexible plates was first called **aniline printing,** because the inks used contained dyes derived from aniline oils. The dyes were dissolved in spirits to provide a very quick-drying ink. This combination of inexpensive plate and quick-drying ink, along with a simple press, made this method most suitable for certain package-printing applications. For example, near the beginning of the twentieth century such a press was used with a bag machine to permit making and printing bags in a continuous operation. By the 1940s, a wide variety of food packaging materials was being printed by the aniline process.

NEW PACKAGING MATERIALS

The new material that started the revolution in modern packaging and at the same time gave a tremendous boost to aniline (flexographic) printing was **cellophane.** Coming into widespread use as a packaging material in the early 1930s, this clear, nonabsorbent film was very well suited to aniline printing. The quick-drying aniline inks, with some modifications, and especially after the development of opaque aniline inks, proved to be excellent for this new material and others that came along, such as acetate film, polyesters, and polyethylene. Thus aniline printing and the packaging industry helped each other flourish, and both have made many technological advances.

FLEXOGRAPHY

But one factor inhibited the growth of aniline printing: its name. The coal-tar source of aniline inks was erroneously believed to be harmful to food products. Although a federal bureau officially confirmed the acceptability of aniline inks in 1949, the name continued to have an unfavorable import. Then the packaging industry, urged on by Franklin Moss of Mosstype Corporation, decided to take action. A committee was formed to rename the printing process, and in 1952 the term "flexography" was born. It quickly attained worldwide acceptance.

Flexography, then, is a method of direct rotary printing using flexible raised-image printing plates and rapid-drying fluid inks.

Flexography is one of the major processes used for package printing. Its simple inking system, which contrasts with the train of many ink rollers required to knead and spread the heavier-consistency inks of standard letterpress and lithography, is one of the features making it attractive to other industries, such as newspapers and business forms, as well as to packaging. And platemaking costs are economical, especially in contrast with those of rotogravure cylinder-making.

THE STAGES OF FLEXOGRAPHIC PRODUCTION

Typesetting

Sometimes (but rarely nowadays) the rubber plates of flexography are molded from a typeform made up of metal type and pictorial engravings. The image carriers of flexography, and of other printing processes as well, are now usually made from films that are a pattern

Phototypesetting using a keyboard and video screen has become the standard in the industry.

of the original artwork—both written and illustration copy.

To start with, two-dimensional type—press-on, strike-on (typewriter), or other, but most commonly phototypeset—has almost totally replaced three-dimensional type. Phototypesetting is done at a keyboard that makes an electronic record of characters and typographic instructions. This material can be viewed on a video screen, edited, and supplied with formatting instructions. Output of the phototypesetter is typically a **galley**—typeset material on photographic paper.

Copy Preparation and Image Assembly

For material consisting only of type and other **line images**—illustrations made up of only solid lines or areas—the images are glued in place with hot wax or rubber cement on a base sheet of white illustration board, paper, or Mylar. This is called a **paste-up,** and is often referred to as camera-ready art. A photographic film negative is made of the paste-up and is then used as a pattern for platemaking.

Development of Flexography   13

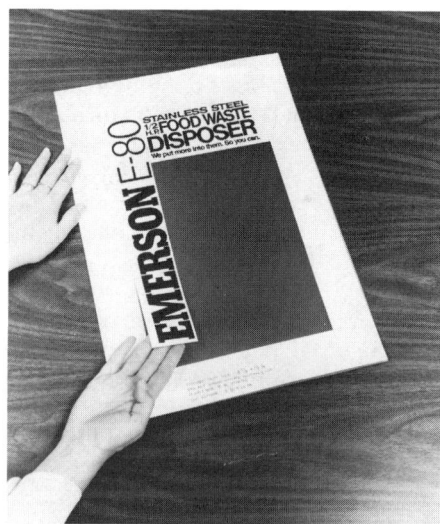

This paste-up for the front of a flexo-printed box contains phototype and a large area (shown here as black) where a photograph will print.

Continuous-tone images—illustrations such as photographs that have variations of tone from black through shades of gray to white—introduce a complication. Flexography, like all other printing processes except gravure, cannot apply different thicknesses of ink to different parts of the image. Therefore the continuous-tone art must

Continuous-tone copy appears to contain tones of light and dark, but it contains solid color (dots) only.

14 Flexography Primer

be converted to another form to be printed. The most common technique is to produce a **halftone** negative of the continuous-tone image in an operation called **screening.** This is done by rephotographing it with a process camera onto high-contrast film through a special film screen called a **halftone screen.** The screen breaks it up into tiny dots equally spaced center-to-center but varying in size according to the darkness of the tone required. When printed, the image will resemble the original, with the smaller dots producing light shades of gray, or highlight areas, and the larger dots dark shades of gray, or shadow areas.

Full color images introduce further complications. Each different-colored ink used in reproducing an image requires a separate printing plate, and therefore a separate pattern film. When transparent inks are used, inks of different colors printed over each other produce still other colors, so that generally only three colored inks are required to produce full-color illustrations. These inks are cyan, magenta, and yellow and are referred to as **process inks.** They are often printed along with black to produce process color, or **full-color printing.** The original colored illustrations are photographed through three different-colored filters to produce negative or positive films for the color plates, a process called **color separation.** Color

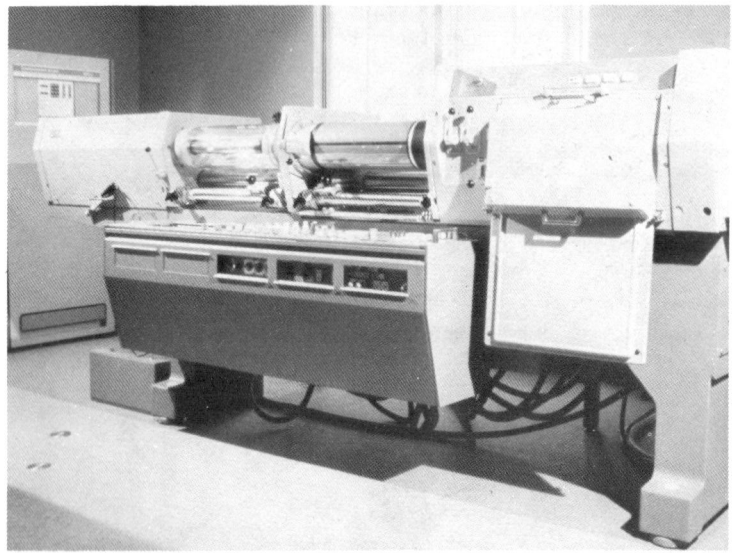

A laser scanner uses light beams, color filters, rotating drums, and electronics to scan and color separate full-color copy.

separation was originally done with a camera, and the screening was also done with the camera, usually as a separate operation. A **laser scanner** is now most often used to color-separate and screen, almost always in one operation.

Platemaking

The films are used as patterns for the process of platemaking. Plates can be made from either natural or synthetic rubber or a flexible material called photopolymer. A rubber plate is produced in a mold made from a metal engraving produced using the pattern film and a photochemical process. A photopolymer plate is produced from the pattern film by a photochemical process acting directly on the plate material.

The flexible plates are attached onto the plate cylinder or cylinders of the press. A multicolor press has a printing unit for each color with its own inking cylinder(s) and plate cylinder. There may also be an individual impression cylinder for each unit, or one common impression cylinder for all. Some flexographic presses are fed from individual sheets (when the substrate is corrugated board, metal, glass, or wood, for example); but usually they are fed from rolls—of paper, foil, polyethylene, cellophane, Mylar, vinyl, fabric, or the like.

Finishing

What follows a printing operation in any printing process depends on the nature of the product. Folding is a common operation, whether folding paper into book sections or corrugated board into cartons. Flexographic printing, being strongly associated with packaging, may be followed by a manufacturing operation such as bagmaking, paper box folding, or diecutting, all of which are in the category of finishing operations called **converting.** These may be done in-line with the printing operation or separately. Rollfed flexographic printing is often followed by rewinding of the web at the end of the press for later use elsewhere.

ADVANTAGES OF FLEXOGRAPHY

From its inception as a kind of mechanized rubber-stamp printing, flexography has developed into an advanced technology that serves ever more effectively its specialized fields. It does this by maintaining the basic characteristics that set it apart—its flexible plate and simple, quick-drying inking system—while improving on their details. New plate materials, new inks (including metallic inks), many press improvements, and new drying methods permit flexography to produce good quality full-color printing on a wide variety of surfaces and a rapidly enlarging range of products.

2 Image Preparation

Image Preparation

PRODUCTION STEPS

Producing a printed piece involves a series of reproduction operations so interdependent and so often overlapping that the final operations of converting, finishing, and delivery to the customer can only be successful to the extent that the beginning operations of design and art and copy preparation are planned with those final steps in mind. A typical flexographic printed piece begins with writing and editing, and progresses through graphic design, typesetting, proofreading, art and copy preparation, graphic arts photography, film image assembly, platemaking, mounting and proofing, presswork, converting and finishing, and finally, delivery to the customer.

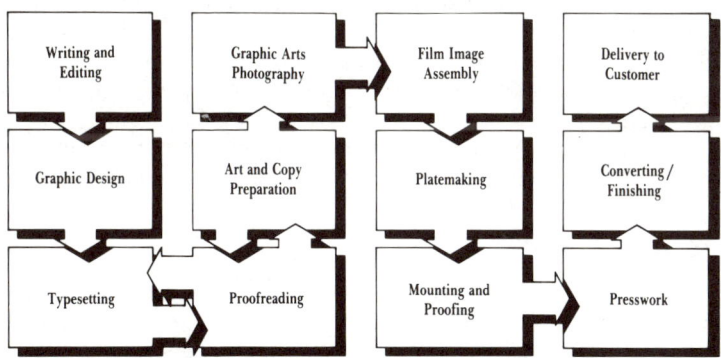

Producing a printed piece.

Many of the steps for preparing art and copy for the flexographic printing process are the same as those for gravure, letterpress, lithography, and screen printing. The first and most important step is planning. A successfully printed high-quality piece demands thorough job planning, and planning demands that the constraints of budget, time, and the reproduction process be evaluated before the job is begun. Once the need for the printed piece is established, the limiting factors of the job must be defined. In analyzing a printing job the following questions should be answered. Since flexography most often prints packaging, the questions that follow are posed with the production of a package in mind.

Does the client have a particular format or style of package in mind? This includes determining whether the package dimensions can or should be altered, and if the substrate can be changed. Additionally, it is essential to determine if the package must conform to requirements of a packaging line. What type of converting equipment will be used to form, fill, close, or label the package is a consideration when determining the size and type of package needed. It is less costly to accommodate the design to the equipment through early planning than to later find that the piece or package cannot run on the press or finishing equipment available.

What is the purpose of the piece? Answers to this question will help determine format, size, shape, and appearance. If the piece is expected to create product personality, establish brand identity, and focus on consumer benefit, as most packaging is designed to do, then it must be appealing or big enough to attract attention, yet detailed enough in graphics or copy to sell, announce, or inform effectively to accomplish its purpose.

Who will receive it? How will it get there? What are the delivery requirements? It is essential to determine who the ultimate consumer or audience will be for this package. The age, sex, socioeconomic level, ethnic or cultural information, and buying preferences of the market are all important considerations when planning a printed package. It is also important to know the conditions under which this product will be displayed and sold to get an indication of how it must compete with other items in the store.

Shipping and handling requirements are important not only from the standpoint of meeting deadlines and wrapping and protecting the goods, but it should be determined if the item offers adequate convenience in handling, storing, shipping, stacking, displaying, and finally, in consumer use.

How many colors will the job require and what substrate will be used? When the artist is limited in the use of color, he or she can gain maximum impact by using tints of colors and by choosing proper color combinations if more than one color can be used. Using a **tint** means making a given color appear lighter (less saturated) by printing it in a dot or line pattern of less than 100%, or solid coverage.

For aesthetic, practical, and cost considerations, attention must be given to substrate selection. A substrate can represent 50% or more of the total cost of the printing job. Whether film, paper, foil, plastic, glass, cellophane, or any other of the abundant substrates printed by flexography, it plays a significant role in the overall effect of the piece. It is important to know how the ink will appear on the substrate. For instance, if a red transparent ink is printed on a transparent plastic bag that will contain a loaf of rye bread, the ink will appear brownish or "muddy" because light will pass through the ink and substrate, and while you will be able to see all of the contents being purchased, the graphics on the bag will lose their effect or appeal.

Will the finished piece be handled excessively? What will be the end use? This is important and relates to substrate and ink selection. If the item will be frequently handled or reused, such as a catalog, cereal box, or bread wrapper, then a durable substrate is a must. If it will be subjected to extreme temperatures or to chemicals, such as a frozen food box or margarine wrapper, or fading from sunlight, such as a

Image Preparation 21

poster or calendar, then substrate and ink interaction and permanency are important.

What type of press will be used? This is important because some flexo presses lend themselves to close-register full-color work, some are suited for wide-web products such as wide rolls of paper towels, or to narrow-web items such as tags and pressure-sensitive labels. Still others are most accommodating to thick corrugated board. Knowing what type of press will be used will permit the designer to know the press specifications and to produce the artwork to fit the press.

Finally, *What is the budget for the piece?* This is probably the most important question discussed in beginning planning sessions because economic considerations affect almost every other aspect of a printed piece, and may well be the most limiting, and at times, unlimiting factor in the reproduction of the job. Not only must the budget be discussed but one must not hesitate to ask what consequences will result if the project runs over budget, should unforeseen problems or hidden costs occur (e.g., an increase in paper costs, a difficult on-location photograph that requires more than one trip to achieve acceptable results).

LAYOUTS

After the various limitations in planning have been discussed, and a manuscript and any visuals (photographs, drawings, etc.) have been approved, the artist is ready to begin planning the layouts that will lead to art preparation. There are three types of layouts used for all printing processes: (1) **thumbnail sketch,** (2) **rough layout,** and (3) **comprehensive.** Each layout is progressively more precise.

Thumbnail Sketch

A thumbnail sketch is the simplest of all the layouts and is drawn much smaller (often quickly sketched in pencil) than the final piece will be, hence the name. Many thumbnail sketches are produced before the artist receives a satisfactory rendition worthy of expansion.

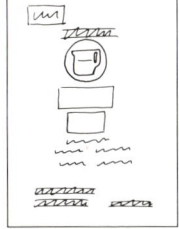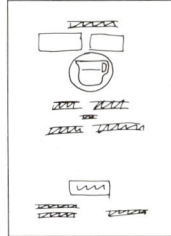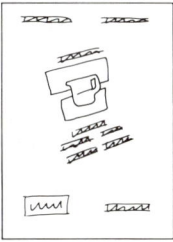

Thumbnail sketches.

Rough Layout

After a particular thumbnail sketch is chosen for development and enlargement, the artist then produces a rough layout. The rough layout is drawn to scale and although the type is not sketched letter for letter, logos and illustrations are recognizable and colors are accurately indicated.

Rough layout.

Comprehensive design.

Comprehensive

In preparing the comprehensive, the artist tries to reproduce what the final piece will look like. In the case of a package, the comprehensive will be formed into the intended package: folded, glued, or assembled in the way it will be when reproduced. The comprehensive serves as a guide for all the art and copy preparation that follows. It is also called a "mock-up."

Typesetting

The designer specifies the type for the typesetter, indicating the type size in **points** (72 pt. equal 1 in.). The **typeface** or style is also indicated. And the line length needed is indicated in **picas**, which is a widely used graphic arts measurement (6 picas equal 1 in.).

The type for flexography is most often set using a phototypesetter that has a keyboard and **video display terminal (VDT).** After the type has been proofread and corrected, the paste-up artist is ready to assemble it, along with the other elements, into the camera-ready artwork or paste-up.

12 pt. Helvetica

ABCDEFGHIJKLMNOPQRSTUVWXYZ ff fi ffi fl ffl
abcdefghijklmnopqrstuvwxyz −[]%*(),.-;':'!?—&
$1234567890

14 pt. Times New Roman

ABCDEFGHIJKLMNOPQRSTUVWXYZ
abcdefghijklmnopqrstuvwxyz ·[](),.-;':'!?−&

18 pt. Goudy Open

ABCDEFGHIJKLMNOPQRSTUVWXYZ
abcdefghijklmnopqrstuvwxyz ,.-; :'!?&

Various typefaces and sizes.

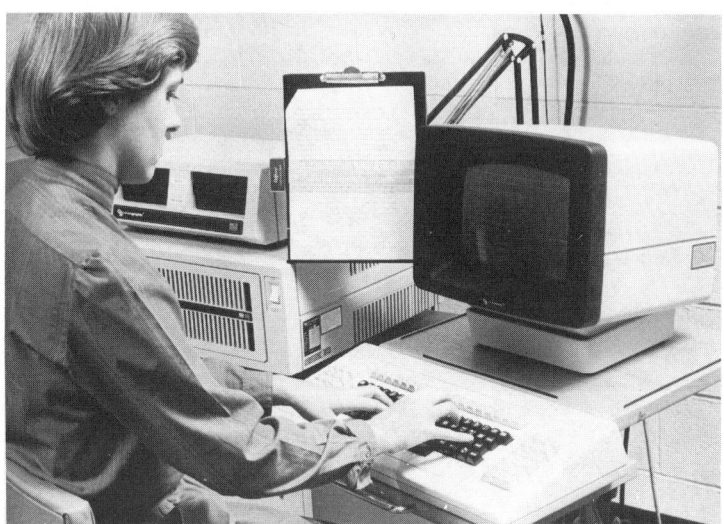

Original manuscript being phototypeset.

Assembling the Paste-up

As mentioned in Chapter 1, the paste-up artist pastes all of the line-copy elements (type, line drawings, etc.) that can be photographed as a unit on a stiff base sheet of white board, paper, or Mylar. Continuous-tone copy is not included on the base art because it must be photographed (halftoned) separately.

24   Flexography Primer

Proofreaders use standard proofreaders' marks when correcting galleys. This galley has been compared to the original manuscript and is now ready to be sent back to the typesetter for correction.

The paste-up artist accurately positions the type and other line images using a T square and triangle.

After the paste-up is completed it is ready to be photographed and converted to graphic arts film negatives in preparation for platemaking and printing.

FULL-COLOR FLEXO PRINTING

As discussed in Chapter 1—Development of Flexography, it is possible in theory to duplicate any hue with just three properly chosen colors in the proper proportions. This principle forms the basis of full-color printing, or process color printing. The three standard inks are cyan, magenta, and yellow. A fourth color, black, is sometimes printed in flexographic printing to increase contrast and further define the printed image. Process inks are considered **selectively transparent,** that is, they absorb certain parts of the color spectrum and reflect others. Only an ink that is selectively transparent can be printed over another to produce other hues. One opaque ink printed over another would simply block out the lower one and reflect the color of the upper one.

To print a color photograph or transparency by flexography, the original must be rephotographed so that individual films can be produced for each of the colors to be printed. As mentioned earlier, the production of one film image for each process color to be printed is called color separation. Color photographs and transparencies are often color separated by an electronic (often laser) scanner, which through the use of rotating drums, beams of light, color filters, and electronic circuitry scans the image point by point, and separates the colors of the original into the four process colors. Once the color photograph or transparency is color separated it is screened (similar to halftoning a black-and-white photo) so that the resulting films can be used to make the printing plates, which will ultimately print dots on press. The scanner produces three pieces of separated, screened film; one for each of the process colors to be printed; four films if black is to be printed.

The transparent inks used when printing process color satisfactorily reproduce full-color copy when combined and overprinted on a white substrate. However, transparent inks present a problem to the flexographer wanting to produce color printing of any kind (single color or full-color) on a transparent substrate such as cellophane or Saran. The contents of the package, for instance, a bag of pretzels, dull the effect of the color of the printing on the package since light passes through the transparent plastic to reveal the contents within.

Therefore, to achieve vivid colors on transparent substrates a layer of white ink is printed under (backs up) the desired color.

26 Flexography Primer

Flat Color Printing

Unlike separating colors and then screening them into dots to print full-color photographs, to produce line art that will print in more than one color that does not touch or overlap another, requires no special camera techniques. When several colors are completely independent of one another on the printed sheet, such as in textbooks where the text type is printed in one color and the headings in another color, all the elements can be glued to one base sheet. To print this **flat color,** or spot color, requires that a separate negative be made of each color. To do this, one negative of the finished paste-up is made then duplicated, and the appropriate areas are marked for each color. This is done by masking out all the elements except those in a given color. **Masking** means to block out or cover over (usually with a special orange masking paper) those images on the negative that you do not want light to expose during platemaking.

Flat colors can be easily printed singly either as tints, solids, or halftones, and are not designed to be superimposed on another ink as full-color process printing inks are.

If flat colors touch or overlap, then the artist will cut overlays for each color and hinge them to the base art with masking tape so they can be flipped entirely out of the way when the base art is photographed. Overlays are usually made of thin frosted or clear acetate that acts as a carrier for peelable red or amber masking material. Each overlay is used to make a separate film which in turn is used to make a separate plate. Each plate will be inked with a separate color when put on press.

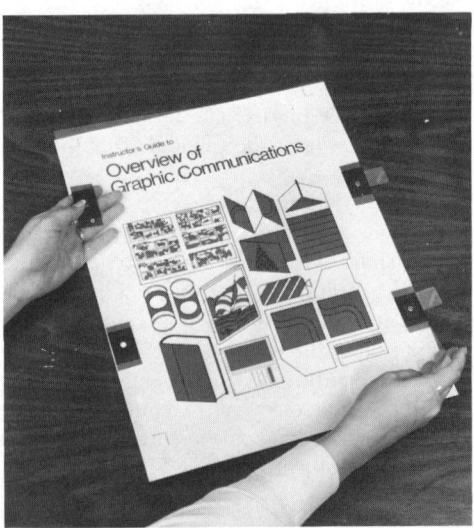

This overlay indicates which shapes will be printed in blue ink (dark areas) within the artwork.

GRAPHIC ARTS PHOTOGRAPHY

After the paste-up is complete, separate negatives are shot of the base art and overlays using a large graphic arts camera.

Often the camera is equipped with an **anamorphic lens,** which allows the camera operator to create distortion negatives directly from the paste-up. The anamorphic lens reduces copy in one dimension while allowing the other to remain unchanged. This is often done

Courtesy nuArc Company, Inc.
Graphic arts horizontal camera with cut-out view of anamorphic lens.

in flexography to compensate for the stretch of the flexo rubber or photopolymer plate once it is wrapped around the plate cylinder. If this is not done, for instance, circular shapes in the artwork would print elongated, or elliptical.

After the negatives are shot of the base art and overlays, and the halftones and color separations are made, the next step is to assemble the many pieces of film in preparation for making the printing plate.

FILM IMAGE ASSEMBLY

Film image assembly, or stripping, is basically the same for flexography as it is for lithography, letterpress, gravure, and screen printing. The film image assembler positions and secures (usually with tape) all of the negatives shot by the camera operator—base art, overlays, and halftones, as well as color separations, to a stable carrier of either paper or plastic. This is called a **flat.**

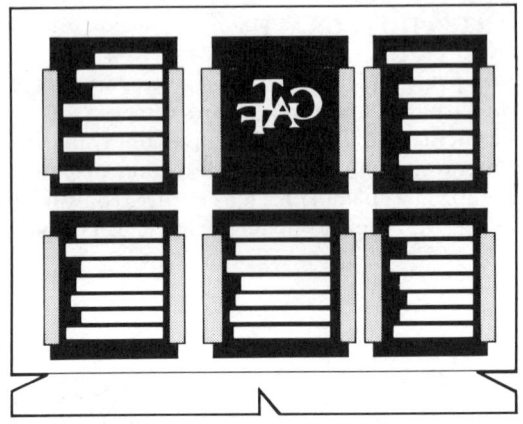

The flip side of a stripped flat showing negatives taped in position.

In single-color package design, the film image assembler could possibly be working with three flats, for example, text, a tint of a color, and a halftone. In multicolor work and in process color printing, the number of flats would increase as each color or type of copy (and the resulting film negative) must be handled separately.

Once the negatives are positioned properly in relation to one another, each flat is ready to be used to produce a flexographic printing plate.

An alternative method of preparing the films for platemaking is to photograph each finished flat that will print in the same color onto a single piece of film. This is called a **composite film.** Composite films eliminate the various thicknesses of film and assembly tape, which could prevent the vacuum platemaking equipment from achieving proper drawdown, or suction. The platemaker will then handle only one piece of film when making a plate.

3 Flexographic Plates

TYPES OF FLEXO PLATES

Once the paste-up is completed and negatives of the art are produced, plates are ready to be made. Flexography uses two types of **relief plates:** rubber and photopolymer. **Rubber plates** are molded from either natural or synthetic compounds. **Photopolymer plates** are made of light-sensitive polymers. Unlike the molded rubber, photopolymer platemaking material is directly exposed to ultraviolet light that hardens the polymer surface. Photopolymer plates can be made from two types of materials: a precast **sheet photopolymer** and a **liquid photopolymer.** Both rubber and photopolymer flexographic plates are flexible, have an excellent affinity for a wide variety of inks, and have the ability to release ink onto many different materials.

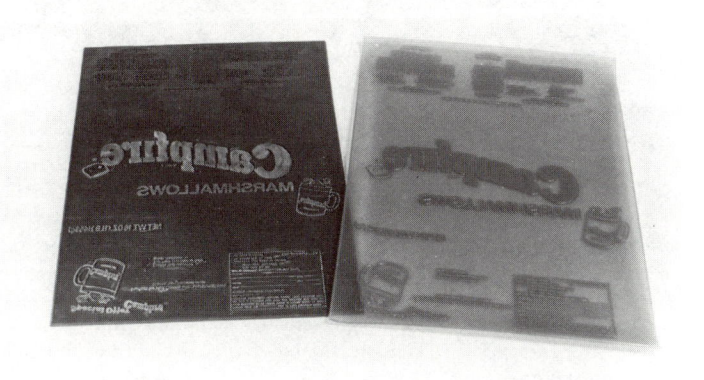

Courtesy Matthews International Corp.
Rubber plate *(left)*, photopolymer plate *(right).*

Additionally, flexographic rubber and photopolymer plates can wear longer than other printing plates of comparable cost, often producing more than five million impressions on smooth surfaces such as polyethylene and coated paper. Hence, flexography is economical. Compared to the even longer lasting gravure cylinders, flexographic plates are less costly to produce. Flexo platemaking is comparable to offset in both speed and convenience, waste is lower than with offset, and water is not applied to the printing plate, eliminating ink/water balance problems found in offset lithography.

RUBBER PLATEMAKING

There are three basic steps in rubber platemaking: (1) making an engraving from the film negative, (2) making a mold, or matrix, from the engraving, and (3) making a rubber plate from the matrix.

Making an Engraving

First, an **engraving** of the image is made from the negative by placing the negative over a light-sensitized metal sheet and exposing it to intense light in a **vacuum frame**—a device that holds films or plates in

Courtesy Matthews International Corp.   *Courtesy Matthews International Corp.*

First a negative is placed over a light-sensitive metal sheet in a vacuum frame *(left).* After the exposure is made, the metal is etched with acid *(right).* This becomes the engraving.

place by means of a vacuum, or withdrawing air through small holes in a metal supporting surface. This exposure photographically transfers the images in the negative to the light-sensitive coating on the metal sheet. (The light hardens the image portion.) Next, the soft, nonimage portions are washed away exposing the metal in the nonimage areas. Then the metal sheet is etched with acid in an etching machine lowering the nonimage areas. This becomes the engraved pattern of the negative, with the image areas high and the nonimage areas low.

Making a Matrix

Next a mold, or **matrix,** is made by placing a sheet of matrix material over the engraving and placing it in the molding press, a machine having two flat platens. Through specific heat, time, and pressure,

Flexographic Plates 33

the matrix board melts and is pressed into the metal engraving. Molding pressure is generated by hydraulic power applied to the bottom table, or platen. The top platen stays stationary.

Courtesy Matthews International Corp.
The matrix *(top)* is made when matrix board is pressed into the metal engraving by the molding machine.

Molding a Rubber Plate

The third and final step, making the rubber plate from a matrix, is also accomplished with the molding press. The relief image is formed on the rubber plate by pressing the matrix against it with sufficient heat, time, and pressure. The plate is stripped from the mold while still warm.

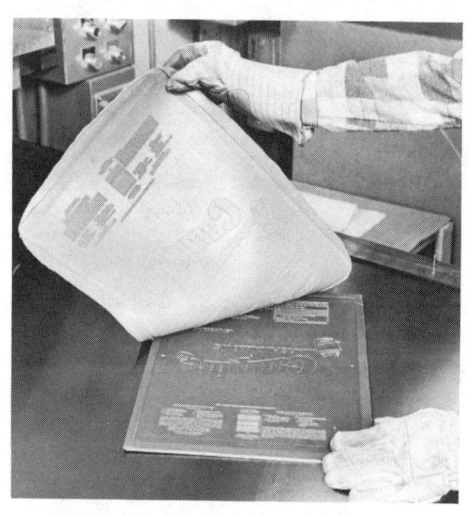

Courtesy Matthews International Corp.
Stripping a warm rubber plate from the mold.

PHOTOPOLYMER PLATEMAKING

A photopolymer flexographic plate is made from either a precast sheet of photopolymer or a liquid photopolymer that is poured to desired thickness and later solidifies to form the plate.

Sheet Photopolymer Platemaking

Unlike the etching and molding process when making a rubber plate, which must first have an engraving made from a negative, the sheet photopolymer plate is made directly from the negative with no intermediate step—each plate is an original made from the negative.

First, the unexposed sheet photopolymer is cut to the desired plate size. Then the back of the plate is hardened, or "cured," by simply exposing it to ultraviolet light (UV) in a vacuum frame. Next the negative is placed over the front of the light-sensitive sheet photopolymer along with a clear plastic vacuum cover. The exposure to UV

Courtesy Alpine Packaging, Inc.

A negative is placed over the sheet photopolymer in preparation for ultraviolet light exposure.

light is then made, causing the polymer to harden in the image areas (or clear areas) of the negative where light enters. In this way the negative serves as a pattern of the image that will be reproduced on the press.

Next the exposed plate is washed out in a processor, which removes the unhardened polymer from the nonimage areas, leaving the hardened image areas in relief. Then the plate goes into a drying unit for further hardening and drying. After washing and drying, the plate is exposed to UV light once more. This postexposure ensures the full curing of the plate.

Courtesy Alpine Packaging, Inc.
Exposed sheet photopolymer being placed in the washing unit.

Courtesy Alpine Packaging, Inc.
Photopolymer plate going into a hardening/drying unit.

Liquid Photopolymer Platemaking

Instead of using a precast sheet of photopolymer, liquid photopolymer can be used to make a plate. The liquid photopolymer platemaking system uses a trough of clear, slightly yellow photopolymer that flows like honey and a plastic backing sheet that adheres to the liquid photopolymer and to the finished plate.

Like the precast sheet plate, the liquid plate is made in direct contact with the negative. The negative is placed on a special flatbed vacuum exposing unit and covered with a transparent film for protection during the platemaking operation. A motorized carriage moves over the length of the bed, depositing a layer of liquid along with the plastic backing sheet. Plate thickness, height of image area,

36 Flexography Primer

Courtesy Matthews International Corp.
Motorized carriage depositing liquid photopolymer.

and hardness can be easily altered for specific jobs when using liquid photopolymer, while precast sheets come in a limited number of predetermined thicknesses.

After the liquid is deposited, the photopolymer is exposed by a hood of strong ultraviolet lamps that are lowered over the plate. This exposure, through the back of the plate, establishes the thickness of the base, or floor, of the plate and permits the backing sheet to adhere to an exposed solid plate. The polymer is then exposed by UV lamps in the base of the exposing unit. This exposure hardens the polymer in the image areas (defined by the clear areas of the negative) on the front of the plate. The unexposed areas remain liquid. The plate is then processed and postexposed in a similar manner to the precast-sheet plate.

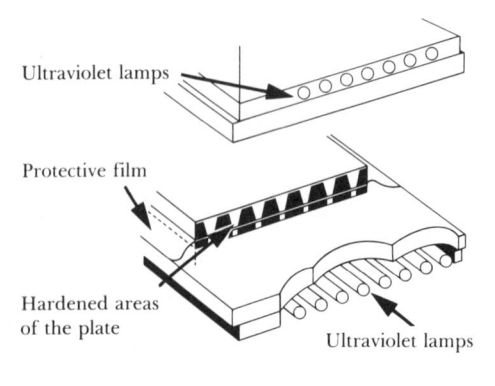

Both a top hood of ultraviolet lamps and those in the bottom table expose the liquid photopolymer plate.

Flexographic Plates 37

Courtesy Matthews International Corp.
After exposure to UV light the plate goes into the processor.

MOUNTING AND PROOFING

In order to determine if a plate will print accurately once on the press, the plate is commonly mounted directly onto its printing cylinder with a double-sided tape called **sticky-back** in a **mounting and proofing machine.** When proofing and printing multiple plates on a single

Courtesy E. L. Harley, Inc.
Machine used for mounting and proofing plates.

plate cylinder, the plates should be staggered across the plate cylinder when possible. **Staggering** the plates, as shown in the following illustration, ensures that a portion of a plate always is contacting the anilox

38   Flexography Primer

Courtesy Matthews International Corp.
Mounting a plate in preparation for proofing.

roll and impression cylinder. This will provide a constant uniform pressure when printing.

If the multiple plates are mounted in a straight line, rather than staggered, there is no constant pressure present. Therefore, when the plate cylinder rotates to the gap or open valley between plates

Incorrect method of mounting plates.

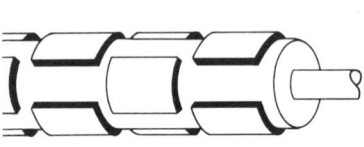

Staggering—correct method of mounting plates.

facing the inking roll, the plates on the opposite side do not receive proper pressure against the impression cylinder. Likewise, when the opening between the plates rotates against the impression cylinder, the plates tend to bounce. Both instances cause irregular printing.

Once attached to the plate cylinder, the plate is inked with a roller and then rolled against a piece of proofing paper that is attached to the mounting and proofing machine's impression cylinder. The plate and proof are then inspected for accuracy, and if approved, the plate is ready to print on press.

For a multicolor or process color job, each plate used to print the cyan, magenta, yellow, or other colors is mounted on its proper plate cylinder and rolled against the proofing paper in the mounting and

Flexographic Plates 39

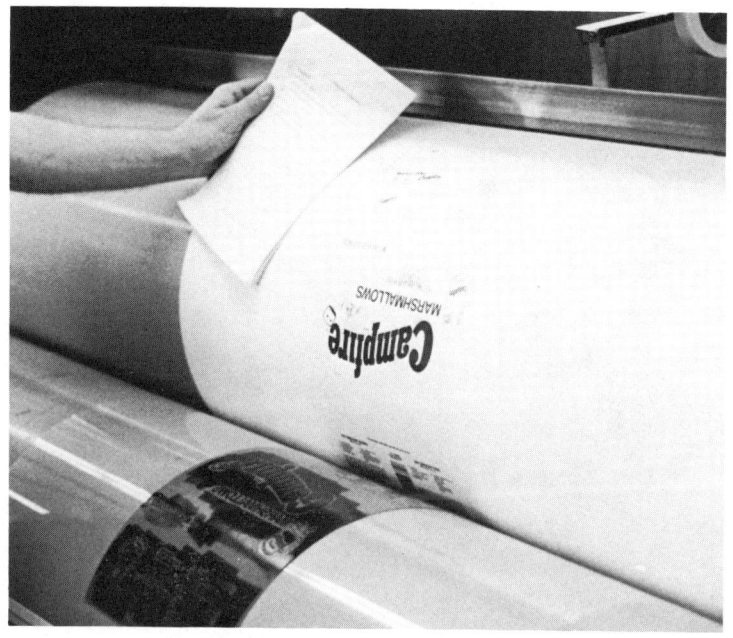

Courtesy Matthews International Corp.
Proofing a plate against original copy.

proofing machine. This allows the printer to see the colors of the piece in proper register, and to make any necessary corrections before the job is printed.

Because in flexography, **makeready** occurs off press, press downtime and turnaround time when changing from one job to another is shorter than for other printing processes.

4 Flexographic Presses

BASIC STRUCTURE OF FLEXOGRAPHIC PRESSES

Most flexographic presses include at least four rollers: (1) a **fountain roll,** (2) an **ink metering roll,** (3) a **plate cylinder,** and (4) an **impression cylinder.**

Fountain Roll

The fountain roll (usually made of rubber) turns in an ink pan, picking up a heavy flow of ink from the pan, or **ink fountain,** and delivering it to the ink metering roll. The fountain roll and ink metering roll are set to rotate under specific pressure against each other. The fountain roll is driven more slowly than the ink metering roll, causing it to wipe away excess ink from the surface of the metering roll.

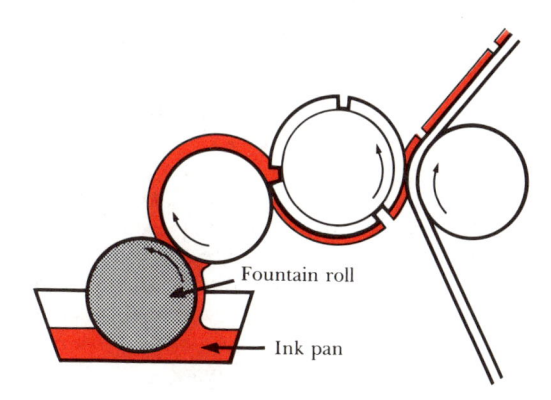

The fountain roll turns in an ink pan.

Anilox Roll

The ink metering roll is often called the **anilox roll,** and is made of either steel or ceramic materials. Its surface is engraved with tiny, uniform cells that carry and deposit a thin, uniform ink film onto the plate. The engraved cells of the anilox roll are so small that they must be magnified to be seen. Since the purpose of the anilox roll is to pass on just a thin, even layer of ink to the plate, the pressure and the speed differential between the anilox roll and the fountain roll are considerable. The two rollers must be set to wipe off excess ink from the surface of the anilox roll and leave it primarily in the engraved cells. This simple, keyless inking system consumes less energy and requires less maintenance than the complex, keyed inking systems of the paste-ink processes. Thus, flexo presses are less costly than web offset and letterpress.

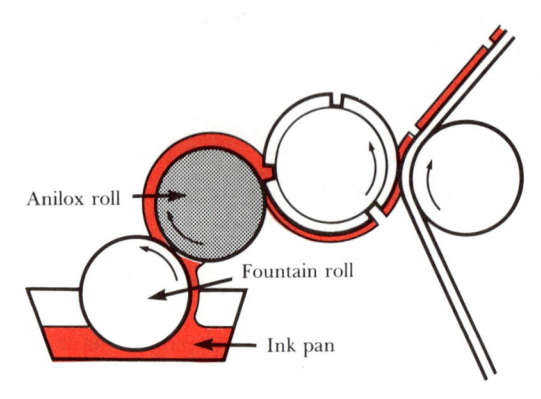

Anilox roll

Fountain roll

Ink pan

Note the anilox roll rotates in the opposite direction from the fountain roll.

Some flexo presses use a **doctor blade,** which supplements the wiping action of the fountain and anilox rolls. Other flexo presses eliminate the fountain roll and have the anilox roll rotating directly within the ink pan. A doctor blade is a metal blade or knife that shaves excess ink off the anilox roll surface, leaving ink only in the recessed cells. A doctor blade is set at an angle opposing the direction of the anilox roll rotation—in other words, set in the opposite direction from which the cylinder is driven. That is why it is often referred to as a **reverse-angle doctor blade.** It provides for a controlled, even amount of ink to be transferred to the plate.

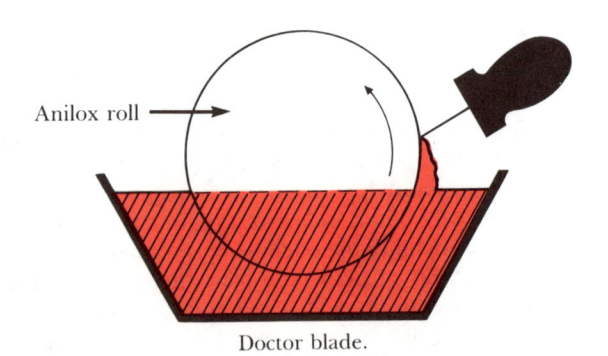

Anilox roll

Doctor blade.

Because of the simple one- or two-roll inking system, which feeds directly and continuously from a reservoir, there are few problems

Flexographic Presses 45

with ink starvation or ghosting of difficult designs, which can occur with the multiroll inking systems. Waste levels are comparatively lower in flexography, as color can be consistent from the first to the last impression.

More common with multiroll inking, mechanical ghosting, or ink starvation, can be caused by the design of the piece. Here the plate was starved of ink in the center of the dark rectangle after the thin black line was printed first.

Plate Cylinder

The plate cylinder is a metal cylinder placed between the anilox roll and the impression cylinder. The anilox roll contacts the plate that is attached to the plate cylinder and deposits its ink onto the raised image areas. The pressure between the anilox roll and the plate cylinder is as light as possible, so as not to crush or push down on the raised image areas of the plate.

Plate cylinders come in various sizes. However, the size of the plate cylinder must be matched to the job. One plate cylinder cannot be used for another job unless the **"printing repeat,"** or circumference of the cylinder, is the same for both jobs considered. For example, in order to print one job—a label that is 6 in. long, and another label that is 12 in. long—using the same plate cylinder, the cylinder must have a 12-in. repeat length. Using a 12-in. repeat, the 6-in. label could be printed two up, or two labels per revolution of the cylinder, and the 12-in. label, one up. This same plate cylinder can be used for any job with a repeat length that divides into 12.

Since one flexo press can handle many different sizes of plate cylinders, hence many different repeat lengths, an existing plate cylinder on a flexographic press can be removed and another easily dropped into position.

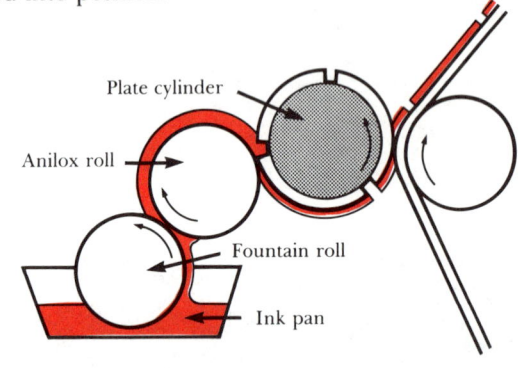

The plate cylinder receives the ink from the anilox roll and passes it on to the substrate.

It is, however, important to keep in mind that the smaller (diameter) the plate cylinder the more the plate will be distorted when wrapped around it. Conversely, the larger plate cylinder, such as a 24-in. cylinder used to print the 6-in. label, may add unnecessary costs to the job, such as extra plates, longer makeready time, and the cost of the larger cylinder.

Impression Cylinder

The fourth roller is the impression cylinder. The material to be printed, the **substrate,** passes between the plate cylinder and the

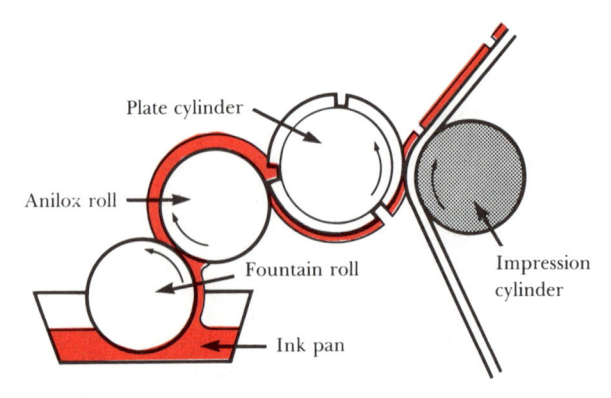

The impression cylinder permits a "kiss impression" on the substrate.

polished metal impression cylinder. The impression cylinder backs up and supports the substrate as it contacts the printing plate. The contact point, or **nip,** between these two cylinders must be just right to give a **"kiss impression"**—the lightest possible impression that transfers the ink to the substrate.

PRESS SECTIONS

Unwind and Infeed Section

Flexo presses generally have four basic sections. Since most substrates printed by flexography are fed through the press from rolls, or webs, the first section of the flexo press is called the **unwind and infeed section.** It is at the unwind and infeed section that the speed of the unwinding substrate is restricted via unwind braking as it enters the press. The infeed draw roll pulls the web into the press to help synchronize web speed to press speed to provide register control. Proper tension control on press also helps to prevent the substrate from wrinkling as well as helps to reduce slack or breakage of the web. Keep in mind, though, that sheets are also fed through flexo presses, as in the case with corrugated board. With sheetfed presses, infeed tension is not required.

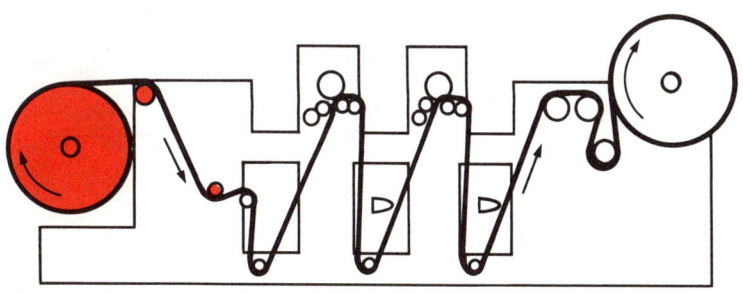

Unwind and infeed section.

Printing Section

The next section of the press is the **printing section.** A single printing station has an inking system, a plate cylinder, and impression cylinder. However, most printing presses are multicolor presses. In other words they have numerous printing stations, each with a fountain roll, anilox roll, plate cylinder, and impression cylinder within a printing section, enabling them to print in rapid succession as many colors as there are stations.

48 Flexography Primer

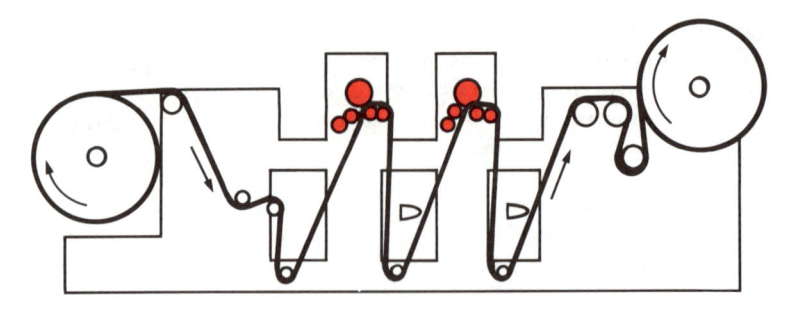

Printing section.

Drying Section

The third section is the **drying section.** Dryers are placed between each color printing station, as well as directly after the final printing station before the substrate is rewound.

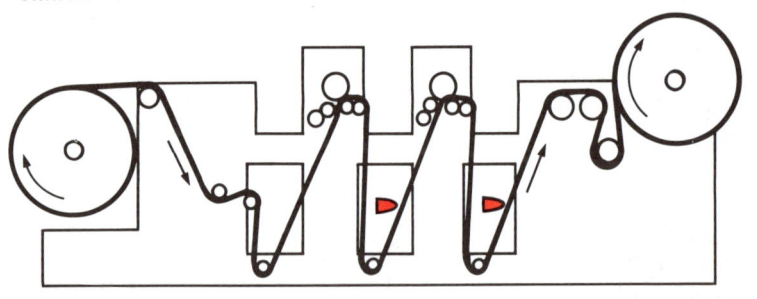

Drying section.

Outfeed and Rewind Section

The final press section is the **outfeed and rewind section.** This section is similar to the unwind and infeed section in that web tension is controlled, yet, while the unwind and infeed section is braked to

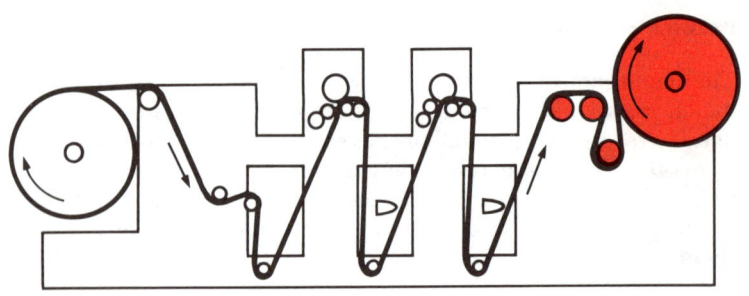

Outfeed and rewind section.

provide tension, the outfeed and rewind section is driven. When rolls are rewound after printing it is called **roll-to-roll printing.** Rolls may be cut by slitters—knives that cut the full length of the web, producing many smaller webs to be rewound.

However, substrates are not always rewound after printing. Rolls can be cut into sheets at the end of the press; some substrates (both sheets and rolls) go directly to another machine that converts them into the intended products, such as folding cartons, envelopes, plastic bread bags, or cereal boxes; hence, at the delivery end of the press one may find a rewind roll, a sheeter that cuts the roll into uniform sheets, an in-line manufacturing operation, or any combination of these.

TYPES OF FLEXO PRESSES

There are three basic designs of flexo presses with respect to the arrangement of units: (1) the **stack press,** (2) the **common impression press,** and (3) the **in-line press.** Each of these types of presses can print from rolls (webfed), and all three come in varying sizes, accommodate narrow or wide substrates, and can print on a variety of substrates. Flexographic presses print webs as narrow as 4 in. (101.6 mm) and less for labels, and as wide as 100 in. (2540.0 mm) for products as diverse as shower curtains to toilet tissue. Depending on the gearing of the specific press and the job to be printed, a flexo press can run at speeds as high as 2,000 linear ft./min. (609.6 m/min).

Stack Press

The stack press has all of its individual color stations vertically stacked one over another. Because of their configuration, stack presses are easily accessible, making on-press changes and maintenance economical. Milk cartons are often printed by stack presses because of the

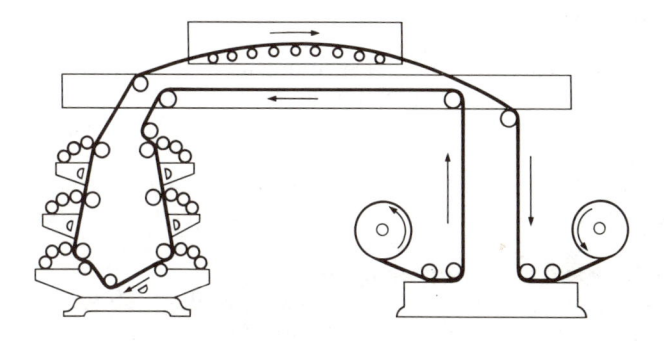

Stack press.

relative ease in changing from one carton design to another for short but varied pressruns. Some stack presses are designed to print both sides of the web with only one pass through the press.

Common Impression Press

The common impression, or CI, press has several plate cylinders positioned around a single, large-drum impression cylinder, which holds or supports the substrate. Because the press is designed with only one impression cylinder, the substrate does not go unsupported

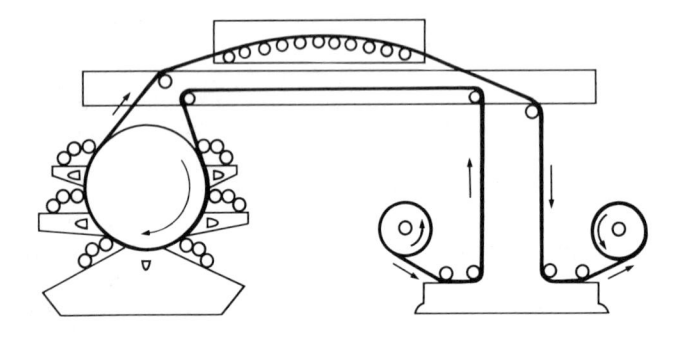

Common impression press.

from one station to another, as is the case with other configurations of presses. This is particularly important when printing on thin, stretchable substrates, such as polyethylene film or Saran, that need some type of reinforcement. The primary advantage of a CI press is its ability to hold excellent **register,** which is the accurate placement of one color in relation to others.

In-line Press

In-line presses contain multiple printing units that are arranged in a horizontal row, each standing on the floor. In-line presses are both sheetfed—such as those used to print corrugated board—and webfed, and frequently are used to print pressure-sensitive labels and newspapers. One advantage of an in-line press is that additional operations such as diecutting can be done following the printing stations on the press. In fact, in-line presses lend themselves well to **auxiliary and converting equipment** that links up to the end of the press. Auxiliary equipment such as web guides, web viewers, ink circulating systems, and static electricity reducers help to better print and handle the substrate on press. Converting equipment performs

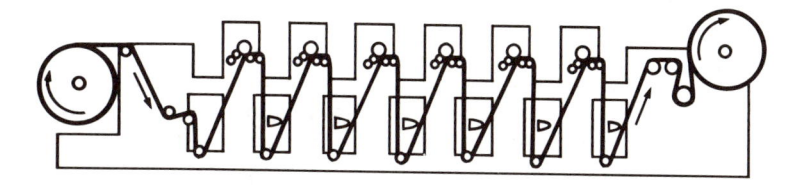

In-line press.

manufacturing operations such as slitting, bagmaking, folding, gluing, laminating, and inserting. These are **in-line operations** because they are performed directly in line with (right after) the printing section. In-line equipment can be attached to stack and common impression presses as well.

TYPES OF ANILOX ROLLS

Central to the flexographic press is the anilox roll, and choosing the proper anilox for the job is important for successful flexographic printing. As previously mentioned, the anilox roll is engraved with tiny cells that hold and transfer a uniform, predetermined amount of ink to the plate. The number of these minute cells varies from 80 to 600 per linear inch (32 to 236 per linear centimeter) on the roll surface. (Generally, the higher the **cell count,** the less ink volume.) Anilox rolls come in various sizes with various shapes of cells. The three basic shapes of anilox roll cells are (1) the **inverted pyramid cell,** (2) the **quadrangular cell,** and (3) the **trihelical cell.**

Inverted pyramid cell configuration.

Inverted Pyramid

The inverted pyramid cell anilox roll is the type of anilox roll most often used. It is recommended for all types of flexo ink applications, as well as varnishes and coatings. The inverted pyramid cell has four walls that are sloped as shown.

Quadrangular Cell

The quadrangular cell is a four-walled, flat-bottomed cell that carries a greater volume of ink for the same cell count than the inverted pyramid cell (the sides are nearly vertical). The quadrangular cell anilox roll is most often used with a reverse-angle doctor blade.

Quadrangular cell configuration.

Trihelical Cell

The trihelical configuration is most often used when applying heavy, viscous coatings. Trihelical anilox rolls have narrow engraved channels rather than individual cells. This type of anilox roll can be used with or without a reverse-angle doctor blade.

The type of job to be printed and the substrate to be used determine the selection of the anilox roll. Line copy that contains little detail and will be printed on film may require an anilox with a cell count of 165 cells per linear inch (65 per linear centimeter). For printing fine type 180-200 cells per linear inch (71-79 per linear centimeter) is reasonable. After selecting the most suitable anilox roll, the proper fountain roll must be chosen. A fountain roll is covered

Trihelical cell configuration.

with either natural or synthetic rubber, and the type of ink that will be used determines which one to use. Some types of rubber cannot resist the strong ink components and therefore are not suitable for fountain roll use. After the proper anilox and fountain rolls have been selected, the fountain roll is set to the anilox roll, which is set to the plate cylinder, which is set to the impression cylinder.

5 Flexographic Substrates

FLEXOGRAPHY AND PACKAGING

"Packaging absorbs nearly half of the paper and paperboard produced in the U.S., nearly three-quarters of the glass, and about one-tenth of the steel and aluminum output."* "Today more than 85% of package printing is done by the flexographic method."†

Why is flexography the leading printing process of the packaging industry? Largely because the process is so versatile—it can print on virtually any substrate. From thin, tiny wrappers for toothpicks, to huge corrugated sheets 12 ft. (3.66 m) wide and ½ in. (12.7 mm) thick, a flexographic press can print the job.

TYPES OF SUBSTRATES

There are five major substrates printed by flexography: (1) **paper** and **paperboard;** (2) **corrugated board;** (3) **film;** (4) **foil;** and (5) **laminates.**

Paper and Paperboard

There are very few special paper requirements for flexographic printing. It is adaptable to a wide variety of papers and paperboards. Most all of the papers that are printed flexographically are made from wood fibers derived from **pulpwood.** Both paper and paperboard consist of the same raw materials, but the distinguishing features of paperboard are that it has greater weight, thickness, and rigidity than paper. With a few exceptions, paperboard has a thickness of 12 pt. (0.012 in. or 0.30 mm) or more. However, some exceptions to this thickness dividing line between paper and paperboard are linerboard and corrugated medium (whose thickness may be less than 12 pt.), and drawing paper (which may exceed a 12-pt. thickness).

One of the simplest and most widely recognized forms of paper packaging that is printed by flexography is the brown grocery bag, made of brown **kraft paper.** Other popular flexo-printed paper and paperboard items that are part of daily living are shopping bags; sugar and flour bags; bags for potatoes, onions, and pet food; paperback books; can labels; pressure-sensitive labels; gift wrap; egg cartons; wallpaper; paper drinking straws; paper cups and plates; paper

---

*Robert J. Kelsey, *Packaging in Today's Society* (St. Regis Paper Co., 1978), p. 42.

†"Flexographic Printing Makes Bid for Newspaper Acceptance," *Editor and Publisher* 114 (6 June 1981):50.

towels, napkins, facial and toilet tissue; checks; forms; ruled tablets; newspapers; milk and juice cartons; and tags.

Multiwall sacks are another type of printable "paper" bag. Multiwall bags incorporate layers of paper and plastic for both strength and resistance to moisture. These bags are often used for overseas shipment of food.

Folding paperboard cartons printed by flexography satisfy a constantly growing market. They line grocery store shelves and are used for everything from bakery products, soaps, dry cereal, ice cream, and pharmaceuticals to toys, retail boxes, hardware items, and beverage carriers.

Rigid paperboard boxes can also be printed by flexography. These include boxes for shoes, cosmetics, cigars, and quality department store clothing.

Corrugated Board

Although there is no printing process that will produce good print quality on the rough, brown surface of corrugated board, flexography has been the best printing process for corrugated since the railroads accepted corrugated boxes for interstate shipments on an equal basis with wood in 1914.

Fluted corrugated fiberboard was first used for sweatbands in Englishmen's hats during the nineteenth century. But an American inventor patented the wavy sheets for use as protection for glass bottles. Another American sandwiched the fluted material between two flat sheets of paper to make the first corrugated container as it is known today.

Packaging manufacturers categorize corrugated by the number of layers of flutes used in its construction. Flutes come in various heights and thicknesses and the number of flutes per foot also varies. One sheet of fluted medium glued to one flat sheet, called a **liner,** is called **single-face corrugated.** Fluted corrugated sandwiched between two liners is **single-wall corrugated.** Two layers of corrugated sandwiched between three liners makes **double-wall corrugated** and three layers of corrugated sandwiched between four layers of liners is **triple-wall corrugated.**

Corrugated is not only used for shipping containers, but as partitions and wraps within boxes to brace and protect merchandise. Food is the largest market for corrugated containers but paper products and durable goods, such as furniture, toasters, irons, radios, televisions, and tools are also big users of corrugated—and they all

Flexographic Substrates 59

Paperboard packaging.

Courtesy Union Camp Corp.
Single-face corrugated.

Courtesy Union Camp Corp.
Single-wall corrugated.

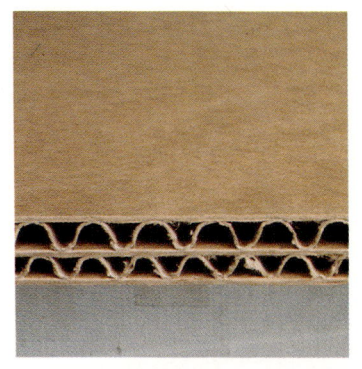

Courtesy Union Camp Corp.
Double-wall corrugated.

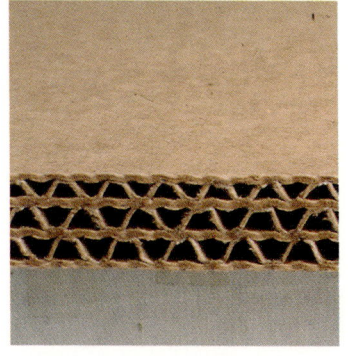

Courtesy Union Camp Corp.
Triple-wall corrugated.

require printing. Corrugated is one of the few substrates that is printed by sheetfed flexography, rather than the more common webfed flexography.

Some colorful point-of-purchase displays that are often seen in supermarkets and drug stores are first produced as preprinted liners by flexo on roll-to-roll presses and then later combined with the fluted medium. Coated corrugated, which is moisture proof and requires special ink to print properly, is now used to ship frozen and fresh produce, such as fresh seafood packed in ice.

Called the "packaging workhorse," corrugated is the most widely used packaging substrate.

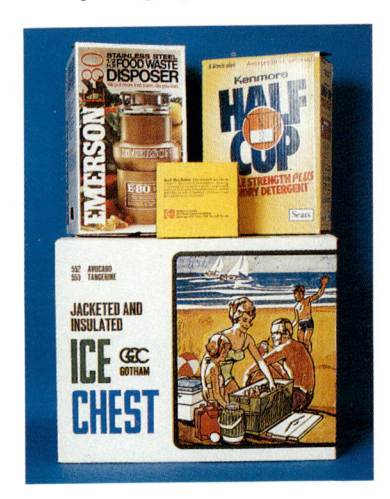

Printed corrugated.

Film

Like corrugated, film substrates are most often printed by flexography. In fact, when the revolutionary film, cellophane, was introduced in the 1930s, it demanded the fast-drying fluid inks that only flexography and rotogravure could print. However, the higher costs of the rotogravure presses and engraved cylinders restricted the use of gravure to large-size, long-run orders.

Polyethylene, which was introduced in the 1950s, is another versatile film that is widely used for packaging. (Polyethylene can be formed into film or semirigid containers or used as coating.) "Poly" film is used to package common items that are used daily; these include fresh and frozen vegetables, fresh and frozen breads, candies, cheeses, meats, baked goods, dry cleaner bags, bed sheets, fabric, shirts, and other retail clothing. Drawstring or diecut handle bags, used to carry retail purchases or used as litter bags, are common items converted from printed polyethylene. Polyethylene has many qual-

Film packaging.

ities that make it an ideal packaging substrate. It resists tears and remains flexible at temperatures as low as 72°F (22°C) below zero. It is also chemically inert so that it does not react with foods, but permits the package to "breathe" by the passage of oxygen and carbon dioxide. And it is impermeable to water vapor so that items packaged in it will neither absorb nor lose moisture.

Along with polyethylene and cellophane, other film substrates such as acetate, Mylar, Saran, vinyl, polypropylene, and polystyrene have been printed successfully by flexography. Disposable medical instruments are sealed in these films and types of foils with the directions and product information printed on the package. This has helped to revolutionize medicine by ensuring that sterilized items remain germ-free at considerably lower cost than if trained medical personnel were required to resterilize instruments between uses.

Foils

Flexo-printed foils are thin rolls of aluminum or aluminum alloy. Foils are printed and used in much the same ways that films are. When used in packaging they are almost always supported by paper or another film. They are used for food wraps, food packages, cigarette packs, as wraps for ice cream, candy, frozen food, dry snack food, and as pouches for tobacco, nuts, and food mixes. Over-the-counter pills and capsules are increasingly produced in push-out foil blister packs. Foil gift wrap is also printed by flexography, and is often adhered to, or laminated to, a paper backing. Aluminum foils are used in fabricating building insulation, as labels for spiral-wound refrigerated dough cans, table salt containers, and oil cans; and in packaging military materiel. Both film and foil, as well as some laminates, are categorized as flexible packaging.

Foil packaging.

Laminates

The whole gamut of foils, films, plastics, and papers can be laminated in endless combinations to achieve properties or meet handling, end-use, or printing requirements unable to be met when using only one substrate. In fact, any type of laminate can be tailor-made, from combining paperboard, polyethylene, and foil to make motor oil cans to combining plywood and wood-grain printed adhesive paper to make table and desk surfaces. There is no limit to the combinations possible, and five or more substrates have been successfully combined and printed. Usually one substrate is printed, then that printed surface is laminated both front and back to another substrate. The top or outer layer protects the printing from the environment, and the inner layer protects the contents of the package.

Some of the packaging products that utilize laminates are snack food, cheese, and meat wraps, and portion packs of ketchup, mustard, soy sauce, and fruit juice.

Since laminated structures are more complex than single-ply substrates, flexographic printers and converters must keep in mind that when combining many substrates with various adhesives and inks, interactions may occur. When working with laminates it is important to check for any odor, taste, or physical property changes that may occur with each substrate after lamination and before printing. Flexographic lamination is more costly than printing a single substrate, so excessive waste must also be watched closely.

Laminated portion packs.

MANY PURPOSES FOR MANY SUBSTRATES

Substrates printed by flexography serve many purposes, therefore the inks used and the type of package designed must serve those same purposes also.

Variety of flexo substrates.

Substrates used for ice cream cartons must be resistant to vapor (moisture transmission) and freezing; those used for boil-in-bag food pouches must resist boiling; still other papers, foils, films, and plastics used for medicine and industrial containers must be resistant to chemicals and drugs. Flexo-printed labels for toys and sports equipment must be able to withstand abrasion. Films made into bags used for snack foods, printed vinyl shower curtains, and film used for garbage bags require good stretchability and pliability but must be tear resistant (have good tensile strength). Christmas ornaments printed by flexo must not crack, peel, or fade with age. Substrates (and inks) used for margarine and butter wrappers must resist oils. And films used to package linens and clothing must be fade resistant (unaffected by sunlight) and retain clarity over time.

6 Flexographic Inks

PROPERTIES OF FLEXOGRAPHIC INKS

Each of the five major printing processes—lithography, gravure, flexography, letterpress, and screen printing—requires specially made inks formulated for the process. Inks used for flexography have two prominent characteristics that together set them apart from inks for other printing processes. They are liquid and quick-drying.

Unlike the paste inks of letterpress and lithography, flexographic inks (as well as gravure inks) are thin and pourable—they flow. This low viscosity, or liquidity, of flexo inks is why flexo presses require so few inking rollers—many rollers are not needed to spread and knead stiff ink before it is applied to the printing plate and substrate.

The quick-drying capability of the inks makes them ideal for printing nonabsorbent substrates such as cellophane, polyethylene, and vinyl. Additionally, flexo inks require simple drying systems. Coupled with relatively uncomplicated press designs, the low-energy hot air dryers on flexo presses keep energy costs down, and the simple press designs keep printing press prices lower than other processes.

All five printing processes have the ability to accurately overprint a given color of ink on top of an already printed ink (as in process color printing). This is called **ink trapping.** The heavy paste inks require a "wet trap"—each ink is wet when the next is printed over it. Since flexographic inks dry so quickly, even between colors, they are "dry trapping," and many trapping/drying problems can be eliminated. Since rapid-drying inks mean higher press speeds, and higher press speeds mean faster turnaround time, flexo-printed pieces have challenged the other four major printing processes on cost and speed.

THE NATURE OF INK

Printing inks consist of three components: (1) **solvents,** (2) **pigments,** and (3) **resins.** Some printing inks also contain **additives** or **modifiers** that impart special properties to the ink. An example of a modifier is wax that is added to ink to make it more lubricant and thus abrasion resistant once printed. The type of solvent, pigment, and resin selected for a flexo-printed job depends on the kind of printing plate, the substrate to be used, the speed of the press, and the end use of the printed piece.

Solvents

The solvent, also called the vehicle, is the liquid portion of ink that carries the coloring component (pigment), dissolves the resin, permits the ink to be handled in the ink pan, and spread into a thin film. When classifying inks by the type of solvent, flexo inks are categorized as either water-based or solvent-based. **Water-based inks,** which mainly dry by absorption, are most often used on highly absorbent paper substrates such as paperboard, kraft, newsprint, or corrugated.

Solvent-based inks, which mainly dry by evaporation, are used on films (cellophane, polyethylene, polypropylene, Saran, etc.), aluminum foils, some papers, and highly coated stock such as that used for pressure-sensitive labels, and milk and juice cartons. The most popular solvent-based ink is alcohol-based ink. In fact, alcohol and water were the principal solvents used in the early days of flexographic (aniline) printing when printing plates were made only of natural rubber. Now flexo plates are made of photopolymers and synthetic rubbers and a variety of solvents are widely used.

Water-Based Inks

Water-based inks have been used successfully to print newspapers and they are particularly acceptable to the consumer because water-based inks don't rub off on readers' hands and there is considerably less **show-through**—visibility of the printing on the reverse side of the paper. Because of less show-through, newspapers are able to reduce costs by using lighter, less expensive papers.

One advantage to using water-based inks is cost. Unlike oil-based inks, water-based inks contain no petroleum derivatives, therefore ink cost does not fluctuate with petroleum shortages. Water-based inks, as well as solvent-based inks, produce salable print with just one revolution of the plate cylinder, resulting in a reduction in waste. They are easily washed up on press also. Newspapers that have switched from letterpress to flexography have found that no **setoff** occurs—that is, when the ink on the printed side of a substrate rubs off on the unprinted side of the next sheet as it is printed, or on the roll substrate as it is rewound. Setoff is a recurring problem in letterpress printing, particularly when printing on newsprint, and its elimination is due to the quick-drying flexo inks. **Blocking,** which is the tendency of a partially dried ink to stick to itself or to another printed surface, can also be controlled with the proper choice of flexo ink.

Ghosting, the appearance of faint replicas of images in undesirable places on the substrate, caused by chemical or mechanical processes other than setoff or show-through, is often eliminated when using flexo inks. This is due to a constant ink film on the plate cylinder in flexo printing.

Water-borne inks also do not pollute the atmosphere as do some solvent inks.

Solvent-Based Inks

Solvents most commonly used in flexographic ink are: (1) alcohols, (2) esters, (3) aliphatic hydrocarbons, and (4) glycol ethers. Some solvent-based inks dry even more rapidly than water-based inks. Solvents (including water) can be classified as normal, fast, or slow. Normal solvents are used for the "average" running speed of a press. Fast solvents are used to speed up the drying time of the ink. Slow solvents are added to slow down the drying time and to prevent the ink from drying on the printing plate before it gets to the substrate.

Solvent-based inks, which are highly suited to printing plastic films, aluminum foils, and glassine, are formulated from alcohol-type solvents and resins. The type of solvent used must be matched to the plate material. Some solvents tend to react with substances in flexo printing plates. (Aliphatic hydrocarbon solvent cannot be used with natural rubber plates because it causes swelling of the plate.) Incompatible solvents/plates causing plates to swell or to pull away from the plate cylinder can be anticipated before getting to the press production stage—solvent/plate incompatibility charts are available.

Pigments

Pigments are the powdered coloring ingredients of ink. When the liquid solvent evaporates from, or is absorbed by the substrate, the solid pigment remains, and this is what is seen on the printed piece. Pigments can be black, white, or any color imaginable.

Early in flexography's history, prior to 1952 when flexography was called aniline printing, coal tar **dyes** (derived from aniline oil) were used as the chief colorant. By 1950, pigments were more commonly used than the aniline dyes, and a new name was needed. The difference between dyes and pigments is that dyes dissolve in the vehicle or solvent while pigments are insoluble. Dyestuffs are still used where maximum transparency and brilliance of color are required. Pigments have better resistance to fading and **bleeding**—when printing inks run into an unwanted area on the printed piece over time. Bleeding is also the migration of ink through the substrate, and in the case of food packaging, into the merchandise contaminating the product. Hence, the pigment (along with the solvent, resin, and additives) helps to determine the suitability of ink for a specific printed piece. Also, the pigment is the most costly component of ink, and the more vivid the color the more expensive the pigment. It is important for the printer, designer, and inkmaker to know the end use and design of the printed piece and discuss the type of ink needed to meet special printing requirements. This rapport is essential in order to keep costs reasonable.

Metallic inks are made of the same components as nonmetallic inks, but the pigment consists of fine metallic powders such as aluminum, bronze, and copper. The metallic powders contain metal in the form of flakes. The luster of metallics is caused by the **"leafing"** of the metal flakes as they float to the surface of the ink.

Fluorescent inks can also be printed by flexography. With fluorescent ink, the thicker the ink film, the more brilliant the color. Since flexography applies a relatively thin ink film, the color strength of fluorescent pigments is limited.

Resins

The resin is the ingredient that binds the pigment to the substrate. In addition to **adhesion,** resins can impart gloss, heat resistance, odor retention, resistance to chemicals, hardness, or film-forming properties to the ink. The resin used will depend on the substrate to be printed, the end use of the piece, whether the ink solvent is water-based or solvent-based, and of course the characteristics of the ink that are desired. Types of resins include: shellac—used in water-based inks on coated board; alcohol-soluble nitrocellulose—used in solvent-based inks to print cellophane and foil; polyvinyl chloride (PVC)—used on polyester films; and casein—used in water-based inks. Of course, resins are dissolved in solvents so they must be compatible—neither must hinder the performance of the other.

Additives/Modifiers

Additives/modifiers improve ink performance. Various modifiers promote adhesion and film flexibility, provide abrasion resistance and slip, and some are antiblocking and antipinholing compounds. **Pinholing** is the failure of the ink to form a continuous ink film on the area being printed. This failure to properly wet the substrate occurs commonly on moisture-proof cellophane and shows up as pinholes in the inked area.

Plasticizers are additives that promote film flexibility. With plasticizers an ink film will adhere to a substrate when it is creased or crinkled. Without plasticizers the ink will crack and flake off when crinkled because the ink is brittle.

Antifoaming agents are modifiers that are used in minute amounts in water-based inks. Water-based inks are chemically similar to soap and tend to foam like soap. Antifoams break up the air bubbles to reduce the foam.

MATCHING INK TO THE JOB

Ink selection is based on the appearance and performance desired of the ink. Appearance, or how the printed piece looks, includes color, gloss, print quality, and transparency or opacity. Performance, or how well the printed piece functions, includes how the ink handles on press, and how well the printed ink does what it is supposed to do on the finished product over time. This includes permanency, adhesion, color retention, abrasion or chemical resistance, proper drying, and how well the ink withstands finishing or converting operations. All must be considered when ordering and formulating the ink.

Inks behave differently on different substrates, and if the printer changes from film to paper or foil, the inkmaker should be consulted. An ink that gives good adhesion, block or rub resistance, and light fastness on one substrate may cost far more than inks satisfactory for another substrate.

In order to meet the often rigid specifications of today's flexo packaging the inkmaker must know if the package will be exposed to sunlight, heat, cold, or moisture; how the package will be handled; if the ink must be resistant to such things as perspiration, soaps, alkalies, acids, alcohol, oil, fat, butter, or adhesives; what the surface to be printed will be; and finally, what type of press will be used—and at what speeds.

Certain printing operations are possible when printing on a transparent film that are impossible when printing on paper or board. Surface printing can be applied to any substrate, but flexographic inks can be printed on the underside of the film, a process known as **"reverse" printing.**

Laminated structures (see Chapter 5—Flexographic Substrates) provide protection against oxygen, moisture, or grease that cannot be achieved with a single material, and it is sometimes desirable to print in between the layers. The ink is reverse-printed on the film before the other material is laminated to it. When the ink becomes sandwiched in between the two laminated structures it must have good adhesion to both substrates and the adhesive used. The wrong ink could **delaminate** (pull apart) the surfaces making the adhesive useless.

Many packages, particularly food packaging, require that the ink and substrate used have no odor. An **odor** or **taint test** is often performed by placing the printed sample in a clean, closed glass jar in a warm oven for a few hours; then they are sniffed for any odor. Chocolate or unsalted butter can also be put in the jar and then tasted to see if there is any ink contamination as there could be in food.

Sometimes the printed ink will come in contact with the product inside the package, such as on a coupon within a cereal box, or a perfume sachet. When this is the case, the printed piece should be immersed in the product for several hours, and then tested to see if ink bleeding or flaking occurs.

Similarly, alcohol-soluble dyes cannot be used in products that would come in contact with alcohol, such as an alcoholic beverage that would touch a printed coaster printed with alcohol-based inks.

Likewise, some pigments bleed in butter, water, or grease. Inks for margarine wrappers, stickers on lawnmowers, bags for fertilizer, or motor oil can labeling must be chosen with the end-use of the product in mind.

Lack of abrasion resistance or even insufficient drying of the ink can make stacked corrugated cartons smeared and unreadable and can ruin clothing when printed matter is brushed against it. Poor abrasion or scuff resistance can also become a health hazard if the poor ink is used to print stacked paper cups where the ink from the outside of one cup transfers to the inside of another.

Because of the wide variety of products that are printed using flexography, troubleshooting is especially complex. As with all printing processes, the ink and substrate interact; problems resulting from this interaction are more conveniently solved by changing the ink than by changing the substrate. However, changes in the ink must be carefully considered so that solving one problem does not lead to another.

INK DRYING

Even though flexographic inks have little **tack,** the sticky or adhesive quality of ink, and dry rapidly by evaporation or absorption, ink drying is usually aided by dryers. Flexographic dryers usually are of three types: (1) hot air jets in a drying tunnel, (2) steam-heated or electrically heated drums over which the substrate rolls, or (3) infrared or ultraviolet curing lamps shining on the printed substrate. Because of the fluidity of flexo inks, drying temperatures are not as high as those used for web offset or letterpress printing. However, as with any ink, the drying temperature of a flexo ink must be controlled. If the temperature is too high, the substrate, such as film, may soften, causing blocking in the roll. If the temperature is too low, the solvent may be incompletely removed, and the soft ink may cause blocking in the roll. Hot ink (and film substrates) can be cooled on a **chill roll,** but it is far more preferable to keep the process under control—to supply exactly enough heat to the web.

In multicolor flexo printing, several colors are imposed in sequence, building ink on the print and affecting the drying. Occasionally the drying rates of the inks must be graduated by selecting the proper solvents so that the inks will trap properly. When this is done, the first-down ink usually contains the fastest solvent, the last-down the slowest.

THE ENVIRONMENT AND FLEXOGRAPHIC INKS

The **Environmental Protection Agency (EPA)** in the United States and similar government agencies elsewhere are restricting the amount of solvents that can be discharged into the air. This promotes the use of water-based inks. New, proprietary resins are being introduced for use on a variety of substrates, and we can expect water-based inks to improve over the years. In addition to its freedom from pollution, water is cheap, nontoxic, and nonflammable.

Although outstanding advances have been made in flexo ink formulations in order to meet a broad variety of special printing requirements, attempts to classify flexographic inks have not met with the acceptance that the gravure ink classifications have.

7 Converting/Finishing

IN-LINE AND OFF-LINE CONVERTING

Following the printing operation, converting takes the printed item and forms it into the intended finished product—the form or appearance is altered. Examples of converting operations include bagmaking, pouchmaking, and boxmaking, which include folding, creasing, scoring, gluing, and sealing, as well as diecutting, sheeting, laminating, and spiral-wound container formation.

Converting can be accomplished either in-line or off-line. With **in-line converting,** the converting equipment is attached to the end of the press, and the substrate feeds directly from the last printing station or drying unit into the converting machinery in one continuous operation. Certain converting procedures also can be done within the framework of the press between color or drying sections. Scoring and slitting are sometimes done this way because the scoring or slitting knives are often attached to the printing cylinders.

In **off-line converting,** the printed rolls or sheets are removed from the press and taken to converting equipment in another part of the printing plant or shipped to a company that specializes in converting. Some printers will store the printed substrate (such as that used for milk cartons) until the client needs the finished item, and only then will convert them. Storage volume is much lower before conversion, as in the case of milk cartons, corrugated boxes, or motor oil cans, than after the container is formed.

FLEXOGRAPHY AND PACKAGING

Flexography is a major printing process but because of its versatility it is also a part of many manufacturing industries other than printing and publishing. Flexography answers the demand for woodgrain laminated furniture, printed shelf paper and wallpaper, and printed rugs, tablecloths, and shower curtains from the decorating and textile industries. The metal decorating industry that produces aluminum beverage cans employs flexographic printing on both alcoholic and nonalcoholic beverage containers. The glass bottling industry prints flexography directly on the glass surface. But the manufacturing segment that has had the greatest impact on the growth of flexography is the packaging industry. Package printing (particularly flexible package printing) has remained the mainstay of the flexographic printing process since the invention of cellophane in the 1930s. While packaging became the catalyst for the growth of flexography over the years, flexography has supported the growth of the packaging industry. This has been largely due to the advancements made in new ink formulations that have low residual odor, no toxicity, compatibility with various laminating adhesives, brilliant color, abrasion resistance, and most importantly, adaptability to print on many surfaces.

Flexo-printed products.

The growth and advancements of packaging and flexography are directly related to the growth and advancements of converting—almost all flexo package printing undergoes at least one converting process. There is specialized converting equipment that encompasses every converting/production operation. Converting machines have become so specialized and such an integral part of the flexo press that it is often possible to print a packaging substrate, dry it, form it into its intended product, fill it with the appropriate merchandise, and seal the package without any break in the action. Of course the speed of the press is controlled by the complexity of the printing job as well as the kind of in-line converting operation.

Cartoning Machinery

Corrugated board, today's "packaging workhorse," is used to package everything from ice-packed seafood to fine china. Because of its rigidity and flutes, it does not wind through the press from a roll. Individual sheets are fed into an in-line press one by one. All of the rollers including the printing cylinders transport the board through the printing and converting operations. After the corrugated is printed it is fed through cartoning machinery, usually a combination slitter/folder/gluer. This converting machine slots, scores, flap folds, and glues the corrugated to produce the finished carton.

Paperboard folding cartons, such as those made for milk and juice, facial tissues, bakery goods, and bottled beverage carriers, are also converted with the same type of cartoning equipment. Additionally, both corrugated and paperboard containers may be diecut to fit around and protect specific merchandise.

Also, fine papers and foils can be printed and then laminated in-line to paperboard to produce specialty retail boxes, fancy holiday boxes, and packaging. Liners used when making corrugated cartons may be preprinted prior to combining them with the corrugated medium. Where even higher quality is required, specialty papers or foils can be preprinted and laminated to the liners either prior to or after corrugation.

Courtesy Union Camp Corp.
Corrugated being slit, glued, and folded.

Diecutting

To diecut a substrate means to punch out or cut out desired shapes using a pattern of sharp knives or metal tools called **dies. Diecutting** is often an in-line process and is used to convert various kinds of papers to envelopes, file folders, greeting cards, pop-up books, and advertising pieces, to name a few. Diecutting is also used to convert corrugated and paperboard to packaging cartons, packaging inserts, and **point-of-purchase (POP) displays.**

80   Flexography Primer

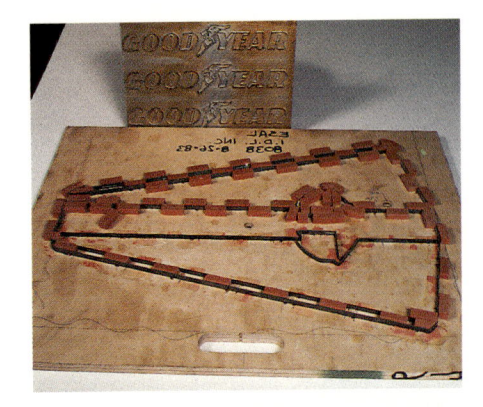

Courtesy IDL Incorporated
Thermal die *(top)* (cuts via heat) used for a decal. Steel rule die *(bottom)* (cuts via pressure) used for an easel.

Courtesy IDL Incorporated
Corrugated point-of-purchase display being diecut.

Labeling

Rolls of pressure-sensitive stock can be printed producing bumper stickers, decals for toys, stickers of all kinds, tags, and labels for pharmaceuticals, shipping, and grocery and retail items. Pressure-sensitive stock can be run through in-line equipment that will diecut, emboss, slit, and perforate, as well as strip away and remove excess material.

Labels that are not printed on pressure-sensitive stock can be glued on press, and both types can be applied to the container intended in a printing/converting/manufacturing in-line process.

Converting/Finishing 81

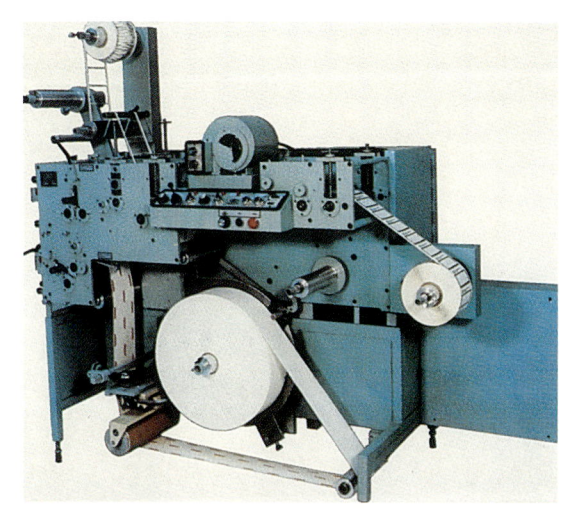

Courtesy Allied Gear and Machine Co.
Two-color flexo label press.

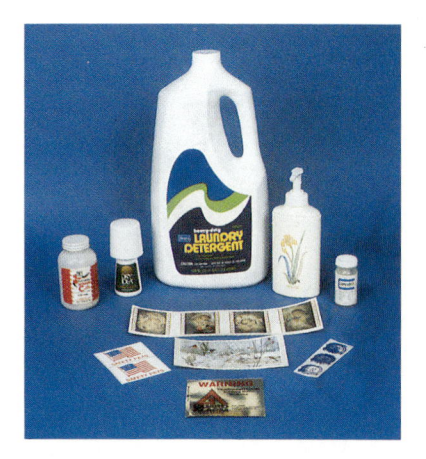

Flexo-printed labels.

Adhesives also can be applied to wide rolls of tape on press. After the printing and the adhesive application, the full length of the master roll of tape is slit, producing narrower rolls with many rewinders rerolling the tape onto individual spools.

Bagmaking and Wraps and Overwraps

Many different kinds of flexo printed paper, plastic, and foil (and combinations of these) are converted into bags, wraps, and overwraps. An **overwrap** is a sheet (usually fed and cut from a roll) of

82   Flexography Primer

flexible material that is wrapped by machines around a particular package. A **wrap** is essentially the same thing but a wrap is formed around the product. An example of a wrap is the printed cigarette package, an overwrap is the cellophane around it. Another wrap is the printed polyethylene around paper towels, an overwrap is the printed cellophane enclosing a box of chocolates.

Courtesy Gloucester Engineering Co., Inc.
Stack press with in-line T-shirt bagmaking system.

Courtesy Gloucester Engineering Co., Inc.
Polyethylene T-shirt bags coming off in-line printing/converting operation.

Bags of every shape and substrate can be printed by flexography and converted at high speeds. Special converting machines form, trim, and glue square-bottom grocery bags, shopping bags, gift wrap bags, fold-close top food pouches, bread bags, and potato and flour sacks from continuous webs of stock. Additionally, many manufacturers receive printed roll stock from a printer and unwind it into converting equipment, which first forms the bag or pouch and then fills and closes the package. This is referred to as a **form-fill-seal** operation, and is particularly common in the food packaging industry, where sanitary conditions and government regulations of packaging must be met.

Coating, Laminating, and Heat Sealing

Coating alters the surface appearance of the substrate but not necessarily the form. **Coating** is the converting process wherein waxes, adhesives, varnishes, or other protective or sealable chemicals are applied to the substrate. Coating gives the substrate added physical and chemical properties not unlike the properties given to flexo ink by additives. Coatings protect packaging—they provide moisture and vapor barriers, such as wax on a juice carton. Coatings also are visually functional—varnish applied to an advertising press kit or pocketed folder gives an appealing glossy surface, but it also helps the surface to resist fingerprints, especially on areas that have heavy ink coverage.

Laminating (see Chapter 5—Flexographic Substrates) and heat sealing are two converting operations that often go together. Overwraps, bags, liners, **composite cans,** and pouches are all common examples of laminated structures—and many are heat sealed. **Heat sealing** is the fusing of two or more surfaces under specific heat, time, and pressure. Sterile pouches for food and medical items such as gauze pads and syringes are examples of items heat sealed under highly controlled environments. They are also complex laminations that must provide a barrier against bacteria.

Fertilizer bags, boxes of vegetables in cheese sauce, freshness seals on jars of coffee, and spiral-wound composite cans of salt and motor oil are all examples of items laminated after being flexographically printed.

8 Flexography's Future

THE SCOPE OF FLEXOGRAPHY

The characteristics and advantages of the flexographic printing process have been presented, but to fully understand the scope of the flexographic process we need only to notice how many consumer products are printed by flexography. Our supermarkets' shelves, freezers, and displays are filled with items whose packages are printed by flexo. We often can find clothes, linens, wallpaper, and furniture all printed by flexography in our department stores. And plastic and paper bags, again printed by flexography, are used to carry these items home.

Throughout a typical day we consistently use and rely on flexo-printed products. From the moment we open our eyes in the morning flexo printing is all around us. Without thinking about it we rely on it to enhance our daily living or merely to help us get through the day's routine.

We may awake to see our bedroom wallpaper that is embossed and printed by flexography. The toothpaste tube we use and the box it comes from are printed by flexo. We pour orange juice from a flexo-printed carton into a glass with a design printed by flexography. The plastic bag that keeps our bread or breakfast rolls fresh is printed by flexography. At work, we find that the control panel (labels) on the photocopying machine, the packages of individual servings of food from the vending machines, and the packets of sugar we put in our coffee are printed by flexography. The string enclosure manila envelope that carries interoffice correspondence is flexo-printed. The carton of yogurt we eat for lunch is printed by flexo. The instructions on the package of the frozen meal we boil for dinner are printed by flexography. And the paperback novel we read before going to bed may be printed by flexography.

Because it is so versatile the flexographic printing process has consistently grown since its introduction into the United States in the early 1900s. According to a recent survey conducted by a survey committee of the **Flexographic Technical Association (FTA)** of Huntington Station, New York, there are approximately 4,650 plants in the U.S. that print by flexography. This figure does not include the book, newspaper, and business form plants that print by flexography.

While flexography has become the leading printing process of the packaging industry, it has recently made some inroads into other printing markets, most notably the newspaper and book printing and publishing areas.

Newspapers and Flexography

The **Research Institute of the American Newspaper Publishers Association (ANPA/RI)** has conducted tests to determine the most suitable printing process for newsprint. The group evaluated every printing process and determined that flexography was the most suitable. This conclusion was reached because flexography met the requirements of: (1) a low-cost press; (2) high-quality reproduction; (3) minimum printed waste; (4) a low-cost plate; (5) minimum personnel needed for operation and maintenance; and (6) adaptability to different types of ink.

ANPA/RI then developed a flexo-type inking system that is suitable for newspaper printing needs. This inking system, which uses an anilox roll, is being incorporated within existing letterpress and offset presses by a small but growing number of newspapers around the country. The system, which replaces the traditional ink fountain and rollers, can be retrofit into presses other than flexographic ones, so newspaper publishers who do not want to purchase entirely new presses can still benefit from flexography's keyless inking system. Additionally, infeed drive units, overhead rollers, and drying components can be added to existing presses.

Some newspapers that are successfully printing with either anilox inking system conversions or full flexographic presses are the *Pittsburgh Press,* the *Easton* (Pa.) *Express,* the *Providence* (R.I.) *Journal-Bulletin,* the *Burlington County* (N.J.) *Times,* the *Greater Buffalo Press,* and the *Washington Post.*

Results are favorable at most newspapers willing to give flexography a try. Individual papers have applauded flexography's versatility. Benefits often mentioned include no ink rub-off on readers' hands and clothing, salable copies after less than ten impressions, faster running time since no ink fountain need be set, no ink misting (spraying) as in letterpress, less energy consumed, and quality equal to offset when press sheets are compared side-by-side.

Flexography is not only making inroads into one-color printing (spot color) of newspapers, but also into printing four-color process work. Greater Buffalo Press has been printing four-color comics and advertisement inserts on a flexo prototype press since late November 1982. Eastern Color Printing is a commercial printer in Connecticut that is printing four-color newspaper fillers and comics using a flexo conversion. Some experts project that flexography will eventually surpass web offset and letterpress as the primary printing process of newspapers in the near future.

However, flexography is not without its problems when printing newspapers. Some papers found that their photopolymer plates swelled because of traces of organic solvents in the water-based inks.

Because of the necessity of flexo's kiss impression and quick-drying ink, others experienced ink drying on the anilox roll or the plate. Color register at top metro newspaper press speeds is still a problem to some. Despite obstacles flexo has been successfully printed and the outlook is optimistic.

Fine Commercial Printing and Flexography

There are those in the industry who believe that flexography also has the potential to make inroads into the lucrative web offset and gravure commercial printing markets. The most often cited of flexo's advantages that permit it to permeate those markets are: reduced waste, off-line makeready, less energy required for press operation, environmentally acceptable inks, and long-run capability. It has been noted that the same predictions are being made about flexography's promising future as were made thirty years ago about lithography's. Additionally, there is no reason to expect that flexography's steady growth since the 1950s will not continue—indeed it will accelerate as refinements in inks, plates, presses, and anilox rolls continue.

Packaging and Flexography

Along with penetrating the newspaper, commercial web offset, and gravure markets, flexography is growing within its stronghold—the packaging market. From 1968 to 1981, flexible packaging shipments increased from $1 billion to $4 billion annually. Demand for high-quality, sophisticated packaging is growing rapidly. This demand comes from the ultimate consumers and is dependent upon their end-use requirements. Preprinted liners used in corrugated packaging is a growing market for flexographic printing. Also the number of paperboard packages printed by flexo has been increasing as designs are becoming increasingly refined and packages are becoming more elaborate.

Flexographic customers are demanding more and more sophisticated graphics on every conceivable substrate to sell their products. Flexographic printers and converters are answering the demand that packaging be safety sealed and the product be secured by providing "over-packaging"—a type of packaging that has been a part of the health-care market for years.

Flexo printers are already doing over $20 billion worth of business per year. Flexography accounts for approximately 25% of the U.S. printing and publishing market with 30% predicted by 1990.

Glossary

A

additives/modifiers—substances that are added to inks to improve performance. Modifiers can promote adhesion and film flexibility, provide abrasion resistance and slip, and are antiblocking and antipinholing compounds.

adhesion—the attachment of a printing ink film or coating to a solid surface.

alphabetic system—a system of writing using a set of letters, or characters, that represent basic sounds.

American Newspaper Publishers Association (ANPA)—a trade association serving the newspaper business and promoting research in the newspaper publishing field and advancement of a free press.

anamorphic lens—a special lens on a graphic arts camera that creates distortion negatives by reducing copy in one dimension while allowing the other to remain unchanged.

aniline printing—an early name (1920s) for rotary letterpress printing that used rubber plates and fluid, fast-drying inks containing dyes derived from aniline oils. Forerunner of flexography.

anilox roll—the most commonly used ink metering roll, made of either steel or ceramic materials. Its surface is engraved with tiny, uniform cells that carry and deposit a thin, uniform ink film onto the plate.

antifoaming agent—a modifier used in minute amounts in water-based inks to break up air bubbles and reduce foam.

auxiliary and converting equipment—equipment such as web guides, web viewers, ink circulating systems, and static electricity reducers that help to better print and handle the substrate on press; converting equipment that performs manufacturing operations such as diecutting, laminating, folding, slitting, and gluing. Such equipment often links up to the end of a press.

B

bed—a flat or level surface on a letterpress press on which the typeform is placed.

bleeding—the spreading of printed inks into an unwanted area on the printed piece. Also, the migration of the ink through the substrate.

blocking—the sticking together of printed sheets caused by wet ink that continues to hold them together after the ink dries. Blocking can also occur within rolls.

C

cell count—the number of engraved cells per linear inch (or linear centimeter) on an anilox roll.

cellophane—a clear, nonabsorbent nitrocellulose film that came into widespread use as a packaging material in the early 1930s. It is credited with helping the flexographic printing process to flourish.

chill roll—a roller on printing presses used to cool the printed substrate and ink film after they have passed through the drying system.

coating—the converting process wherein waxes, adhesives, varnishes, or other protective or sealable chemicals are applied to the substrate.

color separation—the use of color filters to produce, by contacting, or using a camera or electronic scanner, one photographic image for each process color to be printed.

common impression press—a flexo press that has one large-drum impression cylinder, which holds or supports the substrate. Commonly called the CI press, the common impression press has its several color stations positioned around the single impression cylinder.

composite can—a can or drum, often used as a container for motor oil, oatmeal, and salt, made by winding layers of paperboard and laminating them to other materials such as aluminum foil and plastic films.

composite film—in film image assembly, a single film made by contact printing numerous flats for the same color that will be exposed on the same plate. A composite film eliminates the various thicknesses of film and assembly tape, which could prevent the vacuum platemaking equipment from achieving proper drawdown, or suction.

comprehensive—a drawn or constructed replica of what a printed piece will look like, which serves as a guide for paste-up. Also called a mock-up. Comprehensive is short for comprehensive design.

continuous-tone image—copy that contains tones of light and dark areas rather than a solid color only. There is a gradation of tones between the lightest highlight area and the deepest shadow area in continuous-tone copy. A common example of continuous-tone copy is the black-and-white photograph.

converting—any manufacturing or finishing operation that follows a printing operation that takes the printed item and forms it into the finished intended product. For example, converting includes bagmaking, paper box folding, and diecutting.

corrugated board—a substrate made of fluted or wavy paperboard adhered to a flat liner. Numerous flutes can be glued to and sandwiched among many layers of liners. Corrugated board is most often used for shipping containers.

D

delaminate—to pull apart laminated layers of substrates.

die—a pattern of sharp knives or metal tools used to punch out or cut desired shapes in a substrate.

diecutting—cutting or punching desired shapes in a substrate using dies.

doctor blade—in flexography, a metal blade or knife that shaves excess ink off the anilox roll surface, leaving ink only in the recessed cells. Referred to as a reverse-angle doctor blade, it is set at an angle opposing the direction of the anilox roll rotation.

double-wall corrugated—two layers of corrugated sandwiched between three flat liners.

drying section—a unit on a flexo press that drys the ink usually between color stations as well as after the printing section of the press.

dyes—coloring materials of ink that dissolve in tne vehicle or solvent, and used where transparency or brilliance of color is required.

E

electrotype—a relief printing plate that is made by making a hot plastic or wax mold of metal type, electroplating the mold with a coating of copper or nickel, curving the plate into a cylinder, and making it strong and rigid with a cast backing material.

engraving—any pattern that is cut, incised, or transferred onto a surface by hand, mechanical, or photographic methods.

Environmental Protection Agency (EPA)—an independent regulatory agency of the executive branch of the U.S. government. The EPA's mission is to control and abate pollution in the areas of air, water, solid waste, pesticides, noise, and radiation.

F

film—a flexographic substrate. Any thin, basically organic, nonfibrous flexible material usually not more than 0.010 in. thick. Examples are cellophane, polyethylene, Saran, acetate, Mylar, etc.

film image assembly—the act of positioning and securing films to a carrier sheet in preparation for platemaking.

flat—the assemblage of films on a paper or plastic carrier sheet that is used as a pattern when producing a printing plate.

flat color—an ink specially formulated to produce a desired hue, printed either solid or as a tint or halftone, and not designed to be mixed by superimposing on another ink or inks, as full-color process printing inks are.

Flexographic Technical Association (FTA)—a technical society whose membership is composed of flexographic printers and companies furnishing equipment and supplies to flexographic printers.

flexography—a method of direct rotary printing using flexible raised-image printing plates and fluid rapid-drying inks.

fluorescent ink—ink that absorbs light in the ultraviolet regions of the electromagnetic spectrum and radiates it at longer wavelengths. Fluorescent pigments are transparent resin particles containing dyes.

foil—a flexographic substrate. A supported thin metal membrane less than 0.006 in. thick. Above 0.006 in. thick the thin metal is called a sheet.

form-fill-seal—an automatic manufacturing operation where equipment receives rolls of printed material from which it forms the package, fills it with the product, and then seals the finished package. Form-fill-seal is most common in the food packaging industry.

fountain roll—a roll that picks up ink from an ink pan or fountain and transfers it to a metering roll.

full-color printing—printing the transparent inks of yellow, cyan, and magenta, and usually black to produce a full range of all other colors. Also called process-color printing or four-color printing.

G

galley—in phototypesetting, typeset material on photographic paper. A preliminary proof, also called a galley proof. In letterpress printing, a metal tray used to hold lines of hot metal type.

ghosting—the appearance of faint replicas of images in undesirable places, caused by chemical or mechanical processes other than setoff or show-through.

gravure—a printing process that uses a printing cylinder with the image etched below the nonimage surface in the form of tiny sunken cells. The cylinder is immersed in ink, and the excess ink is scraped off by a blade. When paper or other substrates come in contact with the printing cylinder, ink is transferred.

H

halftone—a regular pattern of fine marks, usually dots equally spaced center-to-center, but varying in size, presenting the illusion of continuous tone when seen from a normal viewing distance.

halftone screen—a film screen placed in front of high-contrast film through which exposure of continuous-tone copy is made. The screen breaks up the image into different-size dots so that the image can be reproduced on press. Each dot will be reproduced as a single speck of ink. The resulting image is a halftone.

heat sealing—the converting operation in which two or more surfaces are fused together using specific heat, time, and pressure.

I

ideogram—a picture or symbol used in a system of writing to represent an idea.

image areas—the areas of a printing plate that accept ink and transfer it to the substrate, or in offset, to the blanket. The areas of the printing plate that print the image.

impression cylinder—the cylinder that backs up and supports the substrate as it contacts the printing plate.

ink fountain—an ink pan or trough.

ink metering roll—a roll that meters the amount of ink (or coating) that is applied to the plate. Its purpose is to pass on a thin, even layer of ink (or coating) to the plate.

inking roller—in letterpress, a roller that carries ink to the raised type to effect printing.

ink trapping—the overprinting of a wet ink over an already printed dry, or still wet ink film.

in-line converting—converting done directly from the last printing station or drying unit into the converting machinery in one continuous operation.

in-line operations—manufacturing operations such as folding, diecutting, and converting that are performed directly in line with or right after the printing section on a press.

in-line press—a flexo press that has multiple printing units arranged horizontally, each standing on the floor.

inverted pyramid cell—the most commonly used engraved anilox roll cell formation in flexographic printing. It is literally an engraved, inverted-pyramid-shaped cell that carries the ink or coating within an anilox roll.

K

kiss impression—the lightest possible impression that transfers the ink from the anilox roll to the plate cylinder and from the plate cylinder to the substrate.

kraft paper—a strong paper made from sulfate chemically treated wood pulp, used for paper products such as bags, wrapping, envelopes, and corrugated liners. ("Kraft" is German and Dutch for "strength.")

L

laminate—a product made by bonding together two or more layers of material. Any type of flexographic substrate that is made in this manner.

laminating—a converting operation in which two or more layers of material are bonded together, usually with an adhesive.

laser scanner—a device that uses rotating drums, color filters, electronic circuitry, and beams of light to scan color images and produce tone- and color-corrected color separations.

leafing—the process whereby the metal flakes contained in metallic inks float to the surface of the ink, causing a metallic luster.

letterpress—a printing process that utilizes raised (relief) images as the printing image carrier.

line images—also called line copy, all copy that is to be reproduced but contains no shades of gray (continuous tones) and prints solid (black or color) on the finished piece without the use of a halftone screen.

liner—a thin, flat sheet of corrugated board that is glued on both sides of fluted corrugated.

Linotype—a hot-metal typesetting machine that casts one-piece lines of type to a predetermined length. Matrices are assembled in a line, cast in hot metal, and then recirculated back into storage. The operator uses a keyboard to set Linotype type. Also called a linecasting machine.

liquid photopolymer—a clear, slightly yellow, light-sensitive liquid that flows like honey, which is used to make flexible relief printing plates for flexography. The liquid photopolymer solidifies when exposed to ultraviolet (UV) light during the platemaking process.

lithography—a method of printing from a plane surface (a smooth stone or metal plate) on which the image to be printed is ink receptive and the nonimage area ink repellent.

M

makeready—the preparation and correction of the printing plates, before starting the printing run, to ensure uniformly clean impressions of optimum quality.

masking—to block out or cover over (usually with a special orange masking paper) those images on the negative that you do not want light to expose during platemaking.

matrices—(singular, **matrix**) in hot-metal typesetting, the molds from which relief metal types are formed by pouring or pressing hot metal. In flexo platemaking, a mold made of thermosetting materials, cast from a metal engraving from which a rubber flexo plate is molded.

metallic ink—ink whose pigment contains fine metallic powders such as aluminum, bronze, and copper.

Monotype—a tape-driven hot-metal typesetting machine that casts individual metal types and places them in a line, rather than a solid piece or slug (solid line).

mounting and proofing machine—a machine used for accurately positioning flexo plates on the plate cylinder in order to obtain an off-press proof of the piece to be printed.

multiwall sack—a type of flexible packaging most often consisting of multiple layers of paper and plastic film glued together to achieve strength, resistance to moisture, and the like and to form a shipping sack.

N

nip—the contact point between two cylinders; as between the plate and impression cylinders.

nonimage areas—the areas of a printing plate that do not accept ink and therefore do not print.

O

odor or taint test—a test done when the ink and substrate must be odorless, as in food packaging. A printed sample is placed in a clean, closed glass jar in a warm oven for a few

Glossary

hours and then sniffed for odor.

off-line converting—removing printed rolls or sheets from the press and taking them to converting equipment in another part of the printing plant or to a company that specializes in converting.

offset lithography—lithography produced on an offset lithographic press using a right-reading, planographic printing plate and a rubber-covered cylinder that transfers the image from the plate cylinder to the substrate.

outfeed and rewind section—the section at the end of a flexo press that is driven to move the substrate (either sheets or rolls) out of the press, and, in the case of rolls, to rewind the web.

overwrap—a sheet of flexible material, usually fed and cut from a roll, that is wrapped by machines around a particular package.

P

paper—a felted sheet of fibers, usually made from wood, that is laid down on a fine screen from a water suspension.

paperboard—made of the same raw materials as paper, paperboard has greater weight, thickness, and rigidity than paper (sometimes called cardboard).

papyrus—the forerunner of paper made from the tall papyrus plant, which grew along the Nile. The pith of the papyrus plant was sliced and pressed into matted sheets by the early Egyptians to produce the first writing material to assume many of the properties of paper. The word paper originated from papyrus.

parchment—a fine translucent paper made from the tanned hide of a sheep or goat.

paste-up—an assemblage of all line-copy elements that can be photographed as a unit, which are adhered to a stiff base sheet of paper or acetate. Also called a mechanical, camera-ready art, and/or production art.

patrices—metal dies of raised characters used for making character molds, which are then used to make metal type.

phonetic writing—writing using a set of symbols that represent speech sounds.

photopolymer plate—a flexible relief printing plate used in flexography made of light-sensitive polymers. Photopolymer plates can be made from two types of materials: a pre-cast sheet photopolymer and a liquid photopolymer. Both kinds are exposed to ultraviolet (UV) light during the platemaking process.

phototypesetting—a method of setting type that produces the images on photographic film or paper.

pica—a unit of typographic linear measurement. Six picas equal one inch.

pictographs—simplified pictures or symbols that belong to a pictorial graphic system and are often found drawn or painted on cave walls.

pigment—the solid coloring particles of ink derived from natural or synthetic sources. Pigments can be black, white, or any color. They remain on the printed piece after the liquid solvent evaporates from or is absorbed into the substrate.

pinholing—the failure of the ink to form a continuous ink film on the area being printed, visible as small holes.

plasticizer—an ink additive that promotes film flexibility, so the ink film will adhere to a substrate when it is creased or crinkled.

plate cylinder—a metal cylinder of varying sizes, placed between the anilox roll and the impression cylinder in flexographic printing. The flexible rubber or photopolymer plate is wrapped around the plate cylinder and receives ink onto its raised image areas.

platen—in letterpress, a movable flat surface that is pressed firmly against paper and inked type to produce printing. In flexography, the flat surfaces of a molding press, which exert pressure in the making of molds and rubber printing plates.

point—a unit of typographic linear measurement that is $1/72$ inch. Usually used to measure type height.

point-of-purchase (POP) display—a display of consumer products positioned in a retail store. Point-of-purchase displays usually house or hold the actual packaged product. POPs are often made from corrugated board.

polyethylene—a plastic polymer made from ethylene gas that is used extensively in packaging. Polyethylene can be formed into film (called poly film), semirigid containers, or used as a coating.

printing repeat—the printing length (circumference) of a plate cylinder determined by one revolution of the plate cylinder.

printing section—the section of a flexo press, directly after the unwind and infeed, consisting of all the printing stations of the press. One printing station most commonly consists of one fountain roll, anilox roll, plate cylinder, and impression cylinder; and is able to print one color.

process ink—yellow, cyan, and magenta selectively transparent inks, usually used in conjunction with black, printed one at a time but superimposed in such a way as to print a full range of colors.

pulpwood—wood in various forms as used for the manufacture of wood pulp, such as round wood, logs, chips, sawdust, shavings, slabs, and edgings that has been ground or shredded (where necessary) in preparation for papermaking.

Q

quadrangular cell—a four-walled, flat-bottomed engraved anilox roll cell.

R

register—the accurate placement of one color in relation to others on a printed piece.

relief plate—a printing plate on which the image level projects, or stands out in relief, from the nonimage levels. Both the rubber and the photopolymer plates used in flexography are relief plates.

resin—the ingredient in printing ink that binds the pigment to the substrate. Resins can also impart gloss, heat resistance, odor retention, resistance to chemicals, hardness, or film-forming properties to the ink.

reverse-angle doctor blade—see *doctor blade*.

reverse printing—printing on the underside of a film.

roll-to-roll printing—printing rolls, or webs, of substrates and then rewinding them directly after printing.

rotogravure—see *gravure*.

rough layout—a layout of what a printed piece will look like that is one step above a thumbnail sketch. It is drawn to scale and shows accurate placement of printed elements.

rubber plate—a stretchable relief printing plate used in flexography that is made by heating the rubber and pressing it against a mold or matrix.

S

screening—in graphic arts prepress camera work, the process of converting continuous-tone art, such as a black-and-white photo, into a halftone negative by rephotographing it with a process camera onto high-contrast film through a halftone screen. The screen breaks the image into dots so that it can be printed.

selectively transparent—a property of process printing inks wherein the cyan, magenta, and yellow ink films absorb certain parts of the color spectrum and reflect others theoretically producing all other color hues when combined as in full-color printing.

setoff—an undesirable transfer of ink from the printed side of a substrate to the unprinted side of an adjacent sheet or roll as the substrate is rewound.

sheet photopolymer—a flexible, light-sensitive, precast (not liquid) plastic sheet that is used to make relief flexographic printing plates through exposure to ultraviolet (UV) light.

show-through—visibility of the printing on the reverse side of the paper.

single-face corrugated—one sheet of fluted corrugated fiberboard glued to one flat liner.

single-wall corrugated—one layer of fluted corrugated sandwiched between two flat liners.

solvent—(normal solvents, fast solvents, slow solvents) the liquid portion of ink that carries the pigment, dissolves the resin, and permits the ink to be handled in the ink pan and spread into a thin film. Normal solvents are used for the average running speed of a press. Fast solvents speed up the drying time of ink. Slow solvents slow down drying time of ink and prevent the ink from drying on the plate.

solvent-based ink—an ink most commonly formulated using alcohol-type solvents and resins.

stack press—a type of flexo press that has all of its individual color stations vertically stacked one over another.

staggering—the proper configuration of mounted multiple plates on a plate cylinder. The plates should be staggered around the cylinder rather than in straight banks across the cylinder. This provides uniform pressure between the plate and impression cylinder.

stereotype—a lead alloy relief printing plate made from taking a pasteboard impression of metal type. This impression is curved to become the cylindrical mold for the stereotype plate.

sticky-back—double-sided tape used for mounting flexographic printing plates to the plate cylinder.

substrate—any base material with a surface that can be printed or coated.

T

tack—the sticky or adhesive quality of ink. The resistance of an ink film to being split between two surfaces, as between two rollers, or roller and substrate.

taint test—see *odor or taint test*.

thumbnail sketch—a crude, small layout sketched in pencil.

tint—a given ink that is made to appear lighter (less saturated) by printing it in a dot or line pattern of less than 100%, or solid, coverage.

trihelical cell—a shape of an anilox roll cell that is a narrow engraved channel rather than an individual cell.

triple-wall corrugated—three layers of corrugated sandwiched between four flat liners.

typeface—a unique type design such as Times Roman or Helvetica.

typeform—a term used to describe the formation and alignment of rows of metal type affixed in a metal frame ready for printing.

typographic printing—printing from individual, movable types, using a press.

U

unwind and infeed section—the first section of a webfed flexo press where the substrate unwinds into the press and is braked to provide proper infeed tension and to prevent wrinkling, breakage of the roll, and slack. With sheetfed flexo presses web tension is not a consideration.

V

vacuum frame—a device that holds films or plates in place by means of a vacuum or withdrawing air through small holes in a metal supporting surface.

vellum—a fine cream-colored writing or printing material originally made from unsplit calfskin.

video display terminal (VDT)—a data entry and/or editing/typesetting piece of equipment consisting of a keyboard and a visual screen.

W

water-based ink—an ink containing no petroleum derivatives and a water-soluble or water-dispersible resin.

wrap—a sheet of flexible material formed around a product.

Index

Additive   67, 70
Adhesion   70
Alcohol-based ink   68
Alphabetic system   3
American Newspaper Publishers Association (ANPA)   88
Anamorphic lens   27
Aniline printing   10, 11, 69
Anilox roll   43, 44, 51, 52, 53
Anilox roll, types of   51, 52, 53
Antifoaming agent   70
Auxiliary equipment   50

Bagmaking   82, 83
Bed   6
Black ink   25
Bleeding   69
Blocking   68

Cartoning machinery   78, 79
Cell count   51
Cellophane   11, 60
Chill roll   72
Clay tablet   3
Coating   83
Color, flat   26
Color printing, flat-   26
Color printing, full-   26
Color separation   14, 15, 25
Commercial printing   89
Common impression press   49, 50
Composing stick   5
Composite can   83
Composite film   28
Comprehensive   21, 22
Continuous-tone image   13
Converting   15, 49, 77, 78, 79, 80, 81, 82, 83
Converting, in-line   77, 82, 83
Converting, off-line   77
Converting equipment   50, 51
Copy, continuous-tone   23
Copy, line   23
Copy preparation   12, 13, 14, 15
Corrugated board   57, 58, 59, 60, 78
Corrugated board, history of   58
Corrugated board, uses of   58, 60
Cyan ink   25

Delamination   71
Die   79, 80
Diecutting   79, 80
Doctor blade   44
Double-wall corrugated   59
Dry trap   67
Dryer   72
Drying section   48
Dye   69

Electrotype   10
Engraving   32
Environmental Protection Agency (EPA)   73

Film   57, 60, 61
Film, composite   28
Film, use of   60, 61
Film image assembly   27, 28
Finishing   15
Flat   27
Flatbed press   8
Flat color   26
Flexible packaging   62
Flexographic plate   15, 29
Flexographic production stages   12, 13, 14, 15
Flexographic Technical Association (FTA)   87
Flexography   3, 11
Flexography,
  advantages of   15, 16, 88, 89
  full-color   25
  future of   88, 89
  growth of   87, 88, 89
  newspapers printed by   88
  problems when printing   88, 89
  scope of   87
  versatility of   88
Fluorescent ink   70
Flutes   58, 59
Foil   57, 61, 62
Foil, uses of   61, 62
Form-fill-seal   83
Fountain roll   43
Full-color printing   25

Galley   12
Ghosting   45, 68
Graphic arts photography   27
Graphic communications   3
Gravure   9, 10, 31
Gutenberg, Johann   4, 5, 6

Halftone 14
Halftone screen 14
Heat sealing 83

Ideographic writing 3
Image, continuous-tone 13
Image, line 12
Image area 8
Image assembly 12, 13, 14, 15
Image assembly, film 27, 28
Image carrier 12
Image carrier *See also* Plate
Image preparation 17
Impression cylinder 43, 46, 47
Ink 14, 25, 67, 68, 69, 70, 71, 72, 73
Ink,
   advancements in 77
   advantages of flexo 67
   appearance of 71
   drying of 72
   fluorescent 70
   metallic 70
   opaque 25
   performance of 71
   process 14, 25
   properties of flexo 67
   selection of 71, 72
   selectively transparent 25
   solvent-based 68
   water-based 68
Ink fountain 43
Inking 8
Inking roller 8
Ink metering roll 43
Ink trapping 67
In-line converting 50, 51
In-line press 49, 50
Inverted pyramid cell 51, 52

Keyless inking system 43, 44, 45, 88
Kiss impression 47
Kraft paper 57

Label 80, 81
Laminate 57, 62, 63
Laminate, uses of 62, 63
Laminating 83
Layout, rough 22
Layout, types of 21, 22
Leafing 70
Lens, anamorphic 27

Letterpress 6
Letterpress, rotary 10
Letterpress plate 10
Line image 12
Liner 79
Liner, preprinted 89
Linotype 7
Lithography 8, 9, 31

Magenta ink 25
Makeready 39
Masking 26
Matrix 5, 32
Metallic ink 70
Modifier 67, 70
Monotype 7
Moss, Franklin 11
Mounting, plate 37
Mounting and proofing machine 37
Multiwall sack 58
Mylar 12, 15

Newspaper 88
Newspaper, printing requirements of 88
Nip 47
Nonimage area 8, 10

Odor test 71
Offset lithography 9
Outfeed and rewind section 48, 49
Overpackaging 89
Overwrap 81, 82

Package planning 19
Package printing 11
Packaging 57, 58, 59, 60, 61, 62, 63, 64, 77, 89
Packaging material 11
Paper 3, 57, 58
Paperboard 57, 58, 59, 79
Papyrus 3
Parchment 3
Paste-up 12, 22, 23
Patrix 5
Phonetic writing 3
Photography, graphic arts 27
Photopolymer 15, 31
Photopolymer, liquid 31, 35
Photopolymer, sheet 31, 34, 35
Photopolymer plate 31, 34

Index

Photopolymer platemaking 34
Phototypesetting 7
Pica unit of measure 22
Pictograph 3
Pigment 67, 69
Pinholing 70
Plasticizer 70
Plate,
 flexographic 15, 29
 photopolymer 31
 relief 31
 rubber 31
Plate cylinder 43, 45, 46
Platemaking 11, 12, 15, 31, 32, 34
Platen 6, 8
Point-of-purchase (POP) display 79, 80
Point unit of measure 22
Polyethylene 50, 60, 61
Portion pack 62, 63
Preprinted liner 60
Press 6, 43, 44, 45, 46, 47, 48, 49, 50, 51
Press,
 flatbed-cylinder 8
 rotary 8
 speed of 49
Printing,
 aniline 10, 11
 flat-color 26
 flexographic 11
 full-color 14, 26
 invention of 4
 typographic 4
Printing process 3, 8, 9, 10
Printing repeat 45
Printing section 47
Printing station 47, 48
Process ink 14, 25
Production steps 19
Proofing, mounting and 37
Pulpwood 57

Quadrangular cell 51, 52

Register 50
Register, control of 47
Relief plate 31
Research Institute of the American Newspaper Publishers Association (ANPA/RI) 88
Resins 67, 70
Reverse-angle doctor blade 44

Reverse printing 71
Roll-to-roll printing 49
Rotogravure 10
Rubber plate 31
Rubber platemaking 32

Scanner 15, 25
Screen, halftone 14
Setoff 68
Show-through 68
Single-face corrugated 58, 59
Single-wall corrugated 58, 59
Sketch, thumbnail 21
Slitter/folder/gluer 78, 79
Solvent 67, 68, 69
Solvent-based ink 68
Solvent-based ink, classification of 69
Stack press 49, 50
Staggering 37
Stereotype 10
Sticky-back tape 37
Stripping 27, 28
Substrate 46
Substrate, properties of 64
Substrate, types of 57, 58, 59, 60, 61, 62, 63, 64

Tack 72
Taint test 71
Thumbnail sketch 21
Trihelical cell 51, 52, 53
Triple-wall corrugated 58, 59
Type 5, 7
Typecase 5
Typecasting machine 7
Typeface 22
Typeform 6
Typesetting 7, 12, 22
Typographic printing 4

Unwind and infeed section 47

Vacuum frame 32
Vellum 4
Video display terminal 22

Water-based ink 68
Wet trap 67
Wrap 81, 82
Writing 3

Yellow ink 25